LOOK AT
All that Room
AB●VE THE NET

Wit and Wisdom from a Lifetime in Tennis

TRACY TOWNSEND

First Edition

Hardcover ISBN: 978-0-578-95677-0

Library of Congress Control Number: 2021920735

www.tracytownsend.com
contact@tracytownsend.com

Barkhouse Bay Publishing
www.barkhousebay.com
hello@barkhousebay.com

Special Thanks & Acknowledgments

Dad
*My rock. His wit and sarcasm are with me
always. I know he is with me still…*

Chris & Kevin
My high school rivals that became my best lifelong friends.

Howie Lyons
*Thanks for the suggestion. Tennis
turned out to be a good choice.*

Roger Burdge
*My true tennis mentor. I pretty much
learned it all from this guy.*

Mike Sharman & Larry Thompson
*College coaches that kept me in line when
I was difficult. You put me on my path.*

Robert & Daryl Davis
*Your vision of Seaside has inspired me in
so many ways. It is always with me.*

My wife, Ellen
My love, my partner, my life.

And, finally…
*I hope all pros have protégés. I am so proud of so many
players I have taught. Some I had a lot to do with and some
only a minor role. They have all been very special to me.
I won't mention every name, but you know who you are.*

Contents

Special Thanks & Acknowledgments 3

Foreword 11

Introduction 13

Why Do You Hit the Ball into the Net? 17

Way Out! 18

Don't Be a Rockette 19

Your Shot Sounds Like a Car Wreck 20

Could You Have Volleyed That? (Say Yes) 21

Take Them Out! You'll Never See Them Again, Anyway 22

You Should Have Dove 23

Fun? 24

Winning Is More Fun than Losing 26

Want to Play Better Doubles? Get a Better Partner 27

Hit the Holes 28

The Wind Is My Friend 29

Torture Your Opponents 30

Variety: The Spice of Life and Tennis 31

Good Shot*! 32

Good Try! 33

Too Much! 34

Make Them Prove It 35

If You're Losing, Try to Play Not So Good 36

Go for It! 37

Getting Beat vs. Losing 38

Scouting Opponents 39

Lose the Warm-Up but Win the Match 40

First Return 41

One-Shot Wonders 42

Pick on the Weakness 43

Your Winner vs. Your Weakness 44

Keep Away 45

The Changeover 46

Geometry 47

One-Two Punches Work in Tennis, Too 48

Tennis Is About Time 49

What to Do With an Awkward Shot 50

"Forfeit" a Game on Purpose to Get Back on Track 51

Overheads 52

Shield Your Eyes on Overheads 53

Make Them Hit an Overhead 54

Just Back 'Em Up! 55

Push Lobs 56

Moon Ball It! 57

Say, "I'm Here!" Not, "I Got It!" 58

Strange Lefties 59

You're Standing in the Wrong Place 60

Squat, Don't Bend 61

Set Up in a Good Ready Position 62

Learn to Dance 63

Walk to the Net, Don't Run 64

Volley Position 65

The Statue of Liberty 66

Return Balls Hit at You at the Net as a Backhand 67

Weakest Shot in Tennis 68

Between-the-Legs Volley 69

Behind-the-Back Volley 70

Left Ear Slap Shot 71

Never Go Backward 72

Brace Yourself 73

Where Is Too Far Back? 74

The Point of No Return: Where Is It? 75

Learn to Tolerate No Man's Land 76

I Knew You Were Going to Do That! 77

No Gold in the Alley 78

Play Singles for Better Doubles 79

Move with Your Partner 80

Looking for Something to Do at the Net? 81

What Is a V Pattern? 82

Why Your Serve Is So Bad 83

Place vs. Toss 84

At What Angle Is the Perfect Serve Hit? 85

Hit 10 Serves in a Row in the Box... Every Day 86

Serve & Volley, but Serve Slower 87

Serve with a Twist 88

Vary Your Serve Position to Create Return Issues 89

I Know Where You Are Serving 90

Where Should You Stand When You Receive Serve? 91

Play Pretty 92

Balance 93

"You Messed Up and Did It Right!" 94

Turn, Turn, Turn 95

Slow Down 96

Good Miss! 97

A Good Shot Hit to the Wrong Place Is Not a Good Shot 98

Same Length Swing 99

Backswing 100

Follow-Through or Takeaway? 101

The Myth of "Watch the Ball" 102

Listen to the Ball 103

Do You Really See Contact? 104

What Do You See When You Look at the Ball? 105

Aim Out 106

Quit Hitting It Out 107

Find Out Where Out Is 108

Hit the Imaginary Lines 109

Aim at the White Part 110

Soften Your Grip 111

"Funky" Grips 112

47 Forehand Grips 113

Concentrate on Technique 114

Keep It Low or Add Loft? 115

Mishit Winners 116

Seeing Is Believing 117

"Righter" and "Lefter" 118

Drill Speed 119

The Approach Shot Drill 120

Learn from the Fence Line 121

The Nasty Ball 122

Repeat, Repeat 123

The Alley Rally 124

The 6-Ball Drill 125

Volley Drill 126

Footwork Drill 127

3-on-2 Drills 128

Pick a Spot 129

The Ball Machine 130

Patterns Are a Good Start 131

My Warm-Up 132

Go Watch Live 133

Grunting 134

3 Challenges 135

Shot Clock 136

Coaching from the Sidelines or Stands 137

The Greatest of All Time: Things Change 138

Read The Code 139

Winning Is Easy 140

"Play" like Earl & Pearl 141

See the Good in the Game 142

Parting Words of Wisdom 143

From the Archives

How to Beat the Heat So the Heat Doesn't Beat You 147

Technology and Your Tennis Game 149

Court Partners 151

How to Volley Like a Champ 153

How to Watch Tennis on the Tube 155

It's All in the Racket 157

'Tis the Season to Adjust Your Tennis Game 159

Use the Yellow Ball to Win Your Tennis Match 161

What's Your Style 163

Put a Little Seaside in Your Tennis Game 165

3 Tennis Myths Explained 167

Why Is There "Green Sand" on the Tennis Courts? 169

Tennis Time! 171

Can a Beach Day Improve Your Tennis Game? 173

"Yours!" Really? 175

Tennis Fashion 177

What's Your Position 179

Friends for a Week 181

New Year, New Game 183

Coming Home 185

Get a Grip on Your Game 187

Serve It Up 189

Love Hurts 191

Lesson, Clinic, or Round Robin 193

Aim "Out" 195

Let's Talk About MO! 197

Teach Yourself! 199

A New Era for Tennis? 201

Tennis Season in Seaside 203

Building Your Game from the Ground Stroke Up 205

Court Care for Everyone 207

Spring Forward 209

Hit the Wall 211

Lean In! 213

Which Side Do You Want to Play? 215

When Do I Move Forward? 217

What's New in Your Tennis Game 219

Slow Down! 221

Watch the Pros Play: How to Improve Your Tennis Game
from the Comfort of your Couch 223

Seaside's Tennis Director Commemorates the Program's
Best Moments 225

Seaside Tennis: The Present 227

A Look into the Future at Seaside Tennis 229

Foreword

Tennis is a game, and a metaphor for life itself. Tracy shows us how to win, much of the time, and how to pick ourselves up from our losses, how to learn from our mistakes and how to carry on.

Above all, Tracy teaches us how to have fun, how to PLAY the game. To play well requires work and focus and attentiveness. We need to be able to read our opponents' strengths and weaknesses, as well as understand our own, to compensate for our weaknesses as well as to take advantage of our opponents' weaknesses.

Some of my favorite tips are about relaxing and slowing down, "If you can slow down, it will help you make your shots…if you rush, you'll likely miss." You are "…trying to win the last point, not the first point." (In racing cars, the admonition is, "To finish first, you must first finish" which means you cannot rush your passes, lest they lead to crashes.)

Tracy also helps us understand how to compensate for aging, how to play well, even if we are not as fast as we used to be. These tips are equally useful for those days when celebrating life at the beach the night before may leave us less rested than we should be.

Tracy points out that most tennis games played on Seaside's courts are doubles, requiring teamwork and clear communication, equally true in the game of tennis as well as in work and life.

Tracy offers the reader wit and wisdom on techniques to improve the game as well as continuing reminders that it is a game, to be played hard and to be enjoyed. Tracy's own enjoyment of his work as a coach is palpable. Reading this book will be almost as pleasurable as playing the game itself.

Tracy has been Seaside's tennis pro for 21 years. His contributions to our community have been significant, building a community of enthusiastic players, teaching youngsters how to play a game they can keep playing until they are geezers and helping make tennis second only to beach going for residents and visitors of our town.

Robert Davis
Founder
Seaside, Fl.

Introduction

Tennis has pretty much made my life. Everything has pushed me toward the sport for a very long time. And it has been a great ride every step of the way.

My family lived in Birmingham, Alabama, until I turned 10. Dad was a welder and worked a lot of overtime. I'm pretty sure we were poor, but I really never felt that growing up. Dad loved baseball, and from what I have heard, he was really good. He taught me that same love of the game from a very young age. We lived next to a park in Birmingham, and no matter what time Dad got off work, he would take me there and hit grounders and fly balls to me until it got too dark to see. Those were fun times.

In 1970 we moved to Haleyville, a small, sleepy town in the northwest corner of the state. A friend on my street played a little tennis and took me to play one day. I was hooked. I would get on my bike, load my basket with two cans of balls and my racket, and pedal over to the junior high school, which had a couple of asphalt courts. The net was truly a piece of fence cut to hang between the net posts. To say the least, tennis wasn't exactly booming in Haleyville.

The courts were surrounded on two sides by a 12- to 16-foot concrete wall, and the school sat up on the hill above the courts. When I couldn't find people to play, I would hit on the wall until I was too tired to go on. The hill was important, especially when I first started to play. When I missed the wall, the ball would roll back down the hill to me.

Despite my growing devotion to tennis, I still loved baseball. Dad coached my Little League and Pony League teams, and we nearly always won our division. Actually, as I remember it, we ALWAYS won our division. Dad was a great coach, and that's not just a son talking. In our last year of Pony League, our team won the championship and then played the all-stars off the other teams. We won that game, too. It was always such a fond memory to share with Dad.

The jump for me from Little League to Pony League was tough. I wasn't very big growing up. As a shortstop I could field almost anything hit near me, but the throw from deep short to first became a very long one when we moved up to Pony League. Howie Lyons, one of my teachers and junior high coaches, knew I played tennis. To increase my arm strength for baseball, he suggested that I spend an entire summer playing more tennis. That changed my life.

When I got to high school, I had to make the tough decision to quit baseball and spend all my time developing my tennis. I loved my childhood in Haleyville, but I knew I wanted to move on to a bigger town as soon as I could. Even Dad, with a teary eye, said he thought I could get good enough at tennis to earn a college scholarship. That wasn't likely in baseball, and we probably could not have afforded my education otherwise.

Roger Burdge, the father of one of my friends, had played college tennis and was still very good. I was lucky enough to have him help me through my high school years, and I became a pretty good player. After graduation in 1978, I did get that tennis scholarship and eventually moved on to the University of North Alabama. I am so proud to say I was elected into the Haleyville Sports Hall of Fame.

My college career was a blast. I received MVP awards two of my four years. In 1981 we became the only team at UNA to ever win the Gulf South Conference in tennis. I went 34–6 in singles and 37–3 in doubles that year. I still hold the conference record for most wins in a single season. Upon graduation I was honored to receive another scholarship, this time to the University of Denver to get my master's in sport sciences. Here is where the teaching part really began to take shape. In exchange for my scholarship, I taught tennis and other racket sports.

But fate brought me back home. Mom was diagnosed with cancer, and after graduation from DU in 1985, I returned to Alabama to work and be near her. I took a fitness director job and taught tennis on the side. As the years went on, I taught more and more tennis. And then in 2000, I accepted a job at Seaside in Florida as Director of Tennis. I'm still here today.

Seaside is located on the Panhandle of Florida and is the world's first New Urbanist town, the vision of Robert and Daryl Davis. What started as 80 acres of sand and scrub is now the heart of Scenic Highway 30A, a stretch of beach communities famous for their sugar-white sands. Tennis was fairly quiet in 2000 upon my arrival, and I barely made it through that first winter. Now my clinics and round robins sell out year-round.

I have always known that having fun is the most important thing when teaching tennis. Yes, clients should learn something, but they had better have fun or you will never see them again. When someone learns something new, you can see that spark and the fun they're having. It's a memory they'll keep. My clients return over and over again. Many come several times per year, some only once a year, and some live here. I know virtually every client by their first name, and I rarely forget anyone.

Clients often comment on the funny things I say and the sarcastic methods I use to teach them. I got that great sense of humor from Dad. One of the biggest compliments I get is when a player tells me they "hear me in their head." Some have even suggested that I write a book.

So here it is. With advice from Dad, tidbits from other coaches, and things I have learned from teaching thousands of players for more than 35 years, I give you *Look at All That Room Above the Net*. Think of it as your little book of tennis tips, including more than a few of my favorite "Tracyisms." In one sense, I hope you have heard most of this before. That means you've already received good instruction. But I also hope my fun presentation stays with you and makes you a better player.

You know you need the help, right? Yeah, baby!

Why Do You Hit the Ball into the Net?

After watching me play and lose a match, my dad once asked me that very question. He really had a way with words. His wisdom and sarcasm still ring in my ears today. At the time, I was mad over the loss and had no answer except, "I don't know why!"

"Look at all the room you have above the net," my dad replied. "If you get it over, it could go in. They might play it out of the air even if it was going out. At the very least, they have to go pick it up."

I'm not sure I have won any matches by making my opponent pick up my out balls, but the other two tips have definitely won me matches. And the fact that my opponents do have to go pick up my out ball puts a smile on my face and helps me move on. So, come to think of it, even that tip may have actually won me a match or two. I know I don't hit a lot of balls in the net anymore. Thanks, Dad!

Way Out!

Dad wasn't really a tennis player. He was an old baseball player with a great eye and an even better wit. He taught me that margins in most sports don't really matter. "It was close" means the ball was out. "Just out" means the ball was out. Now that we have shot spot, you can see just how much a ball is out. But does it matter? You need to have a sense of humor to get really good at tennis. Dad said any ball that was out was "Way out!" And he was right. You need to develop a sense of where "in" is and keep the ball in play. Quit hitting it out.

Don't Be a Rockette

I watch players all the time get pushed back onto their back foot by the incoming ball. The other foot goes up and the player resembles a member of the Rockettes. Remember that you're bigger than the ball. You need to get stubborn and lean into it. Don't allow the ball to push you back. Raising your leg and your shoulder only causes a weak reply. And I have seen very few of you who actually look good in your Rockettes pose!

Your Shot Sounds Like a Car Wreck

We have all heard the unsettling sounds of a car wreck. Nothing good ever comes from it. Have you ever realized that your mishits make this same sound? And even when they go in and you somehow win the point, it is unsettling to you and your confidence. Watch the ball! See it as clearly as you can. Make good contact. Quit with the car wreck noise.

Could You Have Volleyed That? (Say Yes)

I like to pose open-ended questions with obvious answers, usually right after a player does something stupid. If you are ever asked this question, don't think too hard on it and simply answer "yes." Look at it this way. If you can step forward and volley the ball, then why do you back up, go the wrong direction, give your opponent all sorts of extra time, and hit a weaker ground stroke? The answer is easy, "I should have volleyed that!"

Take Them Out! You'll Never See Them Again, Anyway

I teach resort tennis, and I call my players "friends for a week." They vacation and play tennis for seven days, and then they leave me. They may come back next month or next season or next year, but many of my clients, I never see again. I kiddingly tell them that if someone is too close to the net, take them out! Since you won't see most of these people again, you might as well hit them.

I don't mean this literally, of course. But you should play aggressively when opponents are at the net. Jam them with balls so they can't get their arms extended or step into the shot. Tournaments and league play absolutely require you to adopt this attitude. You see the pros on television go through the players on the other side of the net. It's just part of the game. No one is trying to hurt anyone, but sometimes you just need to "suggest" they back off a little.

You Should Have Dove

I am kidding! Diving for the ball rarely results in winning the point. You really don't know how fast you are without trying. Run for every ball. If you can't get there, then you can say "good shot." But I see players pull up one or two steps away from shots I think they could have gotten. All I'm saying is give it your all. You're always going to feel better in your defeat if you've done all you can do to win every point. But, please, no diving.

Fun?

Tennis should be fun? Are you kidding? So often I see players on the court in such turmoil. Ladies questioning a line call. Men grunting loudly. The sun is in your eyes. The wind is blowing. Noise is coming from everywhere. Here is the best, simplest, and most important tip in the whole book. You've heard it before, but it is really essential: Have fun.

Let me tell you how important this is to your tennis game. Getting better requires practice. *A lot of it.* It's hot. It's cold. It's windy. Some of your opponents are great, fun-loving people. Some are not. Enjoy it all.

When I first started playing, I remember the fun of tennis more than anything. As I got better and better, I must admit, it sometimes became work. I didn't understand why I got so worked up sometimes about tennis, and then one day my dad told me that I had lost my way. I started out enjoying a well-hit shot. Then I wanted to hit every shot perfectly.

It just doesn't happen.

You have to enjoy the journey. You have to embrace and understand the bad shots so you can enjoy and experience the good shots. You have to have faced off against a "bad" opponent to enjoy the good match with your friends. It really is about having fun. Most of us will not make the pro tour, but all of us can have "that feeling" of a good shot, a good match, a good win.

Learn to enjoy the mishit. And the ball that dribbles over the net on your side. And if your opponent is just a pain, don't you really have something else you can do or someone else you can play? Keep it simple—have a good time on the court. Enjoy the work and the sweat and the noise and the wind. If you are not having a good day on the court, maybe you should go back to your job. Doesn't that sound like more fun?

Winning Is More Fun than Losing

Tennis is a great game. You get a good workout. You get to be outside most of the time. You get to spend time with friends. Remember, though, that the reason we keep score is so that one side wins over the other! And, as I see it, the winning side always has more fun.

I have had great matches that I've lost and great matches that I've won. I admit that the winning ones were more fun. You should admit that, too. It helps you to improve. I didn't get down on myself too badly for the losses, but they did inspire me to practice and boost my game for the next match. And that makes the work involved more interesting.

I always have assumed that when you take a lesson from me that you want to improve… so you can win! Practice makes you better and sometimes that's enough to change outcomes. Work on your game so winning happens more than losing. You will enjoy the game more.

Want to Play Better Doubles?
Get a Better Partner

I t's true. You might think I'm kidding, and yet you know I'm not. It takes two to win in doubles, but it takes only one to lose. I had the good fortune of having a great doubles partner for years, Kevin. I could be looking straight ahead with Kevin behind me, and without even turning around I could almost tell you what he looked like, where the ball was going, and at what pace. We won a lot. I have also played with some really good players (no names mentioned), but I didn't know any of those things about them. And we lost quite a bit.

I tell people to find one partner that you *love* and one that you *like*—and don't play with anyone else, at least not with the expectation of winning. You need to get to know a partner in order to cover certain shots. You need to know your partner's strengths and weaknesses. You need to know how they will respond when the ball is way in front of them or over their head. You need to know where they serve to and how to cover the net for them. You need to know when they are having a bad day, and they need to know when you are having a bad day. I can't tell you how often Kevin carried me on a bad day. But Kevin would tell you I had a few good days myself, too.

Hit the Holes

When you play a doubles match and you look to the other side of the net, what do you see? Do you see two opponents? If that's all, then you're missing something. You also should see four holes to hit into.

One hole is down the middle between the two things you see sticking up out of the court. There is a hole on either side of those two things as well. And there is also a hole either in front of the things you see sticking up out of the court or over them.

I believe you hit where you focus. I laugh when you say you had a good rally and you hit a dozen balls right to your opponent. If you focus on the players (the two things sticking up out of the court), then that is where you will hit the ball.

I try to focus on the holes and therefore run my opponents all over the court. And holes move. Pay attention to what is opening up on the other side of the net, and learn to create your own holes or at least make them bigger.

The Wind Is My Friend

Everyone complains about the wind on the tennis court and how it affects the ball. I say embrace it and have fun with it. I don't know who coined the phrase, "The wind is my friend," but I have heard it all my life and it is absolutely true. Would you rather make the wind your enemy?

You have enough trouble with just your opponent, so don't let the wind get to you. (Or the sun. Or the birds. Or the noise.) There are so many things that can disturb your concentration level on the court, and you simply cannot allow them to bother you.

I played a guy once who after losing the first set decided to slow to a snail's pace. He walked around, picked up balls, and took extreme amounts of time between points and on changeovers. I knew it was simply an effort to make me lose my concentration. The wind is no different. Learn to enjoy it blowing your hair and moving the ball. Learn to soak up some vitamin D while the sun is in your eyes on the serve. Learn to see how pretty the birds are while your opponent is taking forever to get ready. Remember that you could be at work or doing some other unpleasant thing.

Torture Your Opponents

If you know me, you know that I like to aggravate people. (Really, I just like to pick on you to get a smile.) My dad taught me to do the same thing on the tennis court, and it is one of the greatest lessons I ever learned.

Of course, following this advice from my dad rarely put a smile on my opponent's face. That's because he taught me to torture my opponents. In other words, hit them shots they don't like. Make them run and work twice as hard as you are. Get in their heads a little.

My dad's advice was spot on. I found I had a gift for recognizing early in a match what my opponent didn't like. If they liked pace, I would slow the ball down. If they hated spin, that's what I gave them. If they loved the baseline, I brought them in. If they loved the net, I lobbed it over their heads.

You need to develop a variety of skills to combat a variety of opponents. Notice what your opponent does NOT like and torture them with it.

Variety: The Spice of Life and Tennis

We have all heard that variety is the spice of life. It can greatly enhance your tennis game as well. In all of my years teaching, I have been amazed that many of my clients are only good at one thing. They have a good serve. They have a big forehand. They have a great lob. But not many seem to have a good second or third shot. You usually can't win with one tactic. Tennis has just evolved too much for your game to be one-dimensional.

The players with a variety of shots have more success. Developing shots takes time and practice, and that's why so many don't do it. Try this: See if you can add a shot a month or even a new shot every three months. Then look at your game at the end of a year, and I'll bet you are amazed at how much more successful you are.

Good Shot*!

hope you noticed the asterisk. I like to tell my clients, "Good shot! With an asterisk." It's true, shots that win you a point are good shots. But did it go to the right place? Did you step across properly? Was your backswing the appropriate size? Did you hit the shot solidly?

I have always tried to self-analyze as I play a match. For example, would the winner I just hit be repeatable? A shot that goes to a good spot with bad technique might break down. A great-looking shot with great technique hit to the wrong spot might be returned next time. Don't get caught up in one winner. Make sure you can hit a good shot again and again.

Good Try!

You should absolutely hate this phrase. What you always want to hear is "Good shot!"

Words of encouragement like "good try," "good idea," "nice effort," and "so close" *all* mean the exact same thing—you lost the point! The only thing worse is "good hustle." That actually means you ran your butt off and still lost the point!

Too Much!

I love watching someone hit a ball out and say, "Too much!" But was it really too much, or was it actually too little? Lots of things can make a ball go out. Too much pace. Too much angle. Too high. Too open with the racket face. There's also too little follow-through. Too little spin. Too little thought. And too little preparation. I try to get players to look at the whole picture before saying a shot was too much. We all need to find the right balance at the right time, physically and mentally.

Make Them Prove It

Your opponent hits a deep shot and rushes the net. You go crazy (like you normally do) and try for the unreal passing shot. But do you know if this player can even volley? Well, make them prove it. Not once but at least two or three times.

I'm amazed at players who go for nearly impossible shots when it may not be necessary. Sure, it looks better to pass someone, but the idea is to win more points than your opponent. Players missing volleys get frustrated. And how fun is it to frustrate your opponent? Make them prove all parts of their game before doing stupid things yourself.

If You're Losing, Try to Play Not So Good

You have to look at a match in two ways. Sometimes you need to play better to win, and sometimes you just need to play smarter. I'm not telling you to not do your best. But I have played matches where I hit really great shots and still lost. I found in some of those matches, if I tried to *not* hit it so good, I actually won more points.

Some opponents feed off of pace. The better you hit it to them, the better they like it. I found that if I floated some balls back during a hard rally, I would disrupt my opponent's timing. Some players hate a ball that is lofted slowly, deep into the court. For them, I found that my "hack" shot with excessive spin worked very well, so I tried not to hit every shot so great. I believe every player has a weakness. It may seem unlikely that hitting a ball softer can be more effective, but I am telling you that it can.

Go for It!

G reat opportunity exists when you are way up or way down in a game. At 40–love, I feel like I have a free point to play with. That means my attitude changes, and I go for it big time. You should do the same. Try to hit an ace if serving. Or hit another first serve if you miss your first. But go big. If returning, try to hit a winner. Rip it up the line, or hit an incredible drop shot or a topspin lob. These are opportunities for you to blow your opponent's mind and win a game that can really set the tone of rest of the match. Go for it!

Getting Beat vs. Losing

It is one thing to get beat by a better player. A shot too hard to handle or too far away is just a good shot. You shouldn't feel bad about getting beat in these circumstances. However, if you're dumping balls in the net or blasting easy shots out, you're losing. You should feel bad. Fix the problem and stop losing!

Scouting Opponents

When I scouted opponents, I looked for tendencies and weaknesses, noting which shots they liked to hit. Better still, I noticed which shots they didn't like to hit or didn't hit well. But that was just the beginning. There are plenty of other questions to ask. Does your opponent move forward or do they hang back? What kind of serve do they have? How is their second serve? Can they volley effectively? Can they put away an overhead? Answering these questions will give you a big advantage and a lot of confidence in your game plan. Oh, yeah, you need one of those, too.

Lose the Warm-Up but Win the Match

I f I need to hit shots and get loose before a match, I do it *before* the warm-up. Then I use the warm-up to fine-tune any shots I feel need help, but my main focus is on my opponent.

You should pay attention to your opponent during warm-ups, too. Watch the shots they hit and see if there's anything off in their game. Do they spend a lot of time on the baseline or at the net? Does that mean they are really good at the net or are they trying to work something out? If you want to win, you better figure it out. If you are playing someone you don't know, this may be the only time you have to formulate a game plan. Warm-ups don't count toward the final score. Use that time wisely. You are trying to win the last point, not the first point.

First Return

Here's a tip to get a match started in doubles. Always take your first return of the match down the alley. Why? Well, you might actually make the shot and win the point. And even if you slightly miss and lose the point, you have at least planted the thought in your opponent's mind that you are not afraid to try the shot. This can pay dividends later in the match by making your opponent guard the alley a little too much. It also could (or should) open up the middle of the court slightly more. Lastly, it makes you feel better about yourself if you are using the whole court. Making this shot on your first return will give you confidence.

One-Shot Wonders

I loved college tennis, and then tournaments after that. I was constantly amazed at the one-shot wonders that existed even at that level. Some players are so good at one shot that they can have a very high level of success. You even see pro players who can have very good careers with only a huge serve, a big forehand or backhand, or a great volley. But when you figure out how to take that one shot away from them, the success rate falls. Pay attention to your opponent's shot-making ability and devise a plan to avoid the strength. I have beaten many better players who had only one really good shot.

Pick on the Weakness

In doubles, one player on your opponent's side is better than the other player on your opponent's side. Or at least one player is "hotter" than the other. Find out who it is. In singles, every player has a favorite shot, and every player has a weaker shot. Find it.

Use your brain as you play and think about where you are winning points and where your opponent is losing points. Then exploit it. Big forehands that don't go in often are probably not shots that are hurting you. But that doubles partner who never misses is hurting you. That player who stands back on the baseline is either really good at ground strokes or really uncomfortable at volleys. Pay attention and avoid what or who is hurting you or your team. During every changeover, you should analyze what is going on so your game plan stays sound. Think!

Your Winner vs. Your Weakness

Now that I no longer compete in leagues or tournaments, I can tell all the dummies who played me that my backhand was always my strength. But I disguised it well. When my opponents first hit me a forehand, I tried my best to pull off one really scary shot. I stepped in as best as I could and I went for it. I wanted to scare them to death with it. While I knew my forehand often seemed to break down on me, I wanted my opponents to be afraid of it.

My slower backhand, however, had different spins, could be placed anywhere, and rarely ever fell apart. It took me longer to construct the point with my backhand, but it always seemed to really frustrate my opponent because it didn't *look* like a strength. If you play someone who hits the shot back every time with different spins and speeds to anywhere on the court from a particular side, *that* is their strength. It is not the one huge shot that looks scary but goes in one time out of ten. Hint, hint!

Keep Away

Remember the game "keep away" we played when we were young? It mainly seemed to aggravate the one in the middle. It can also aggravate your opponent. I teach players to play keep away from their opponent. Run them around and make them hit while moving. Move them up and back on the court. Move them side to side. See what they don't like to do and make them do it over and over. This is not gamesmanship. It's simply being smart by using a childhood game to your benefit.

The Changeover

Changeovers are meant for you to rest and replenish. But they should also be used to adjust game plan and strategy. Think about what is winning you points. Think about what is losing you points. Formulate a plan for the next two games and then see how that plan has worked at the next changeover. Things change constantly during a match, and you need to know what to do about it. In doubles, get on the same page as your partner. Maybe they have noticed something different. Two heads are better than one, I hear.

Geometry

I liked geometry in school. All those angles and arcs fascinated me, and I remember studying the space between them. I absolutely think about angles and arcs when playing tennis. I try to create space and hit it there as often as possible.

You should think about angles and arcs, too. Angles get your opponent out of position. The arc of any shot can be equally effective. (The arc of your lob is especially important.) And space is maybe the most valuable thing you can create. If you create enough space or open court, you can make just about any shot.

One-Two Punches
Work in Tennis, Too

I'm not much of a boxing fan, but it shares some common ground with tennis. Like boxing, in a singles match it's just you fighting against your opponent on the other side of the net. Like boxing, footwork is instrumental to your success. And like boxing, a good one-two plan is effective.

One, I hit a deep shot. *Two*, I hit a drop shot. Or *one*, I hit a drop shot. *Two*, I hit a lob. Or *one*, I hit wide to the forehand. *Two*, I hit wide to the backhand. Find your own one-two combinations and put them into your game plan. Prepare in pairs. One shot won't get it done most of the time.

Tennis Is About Time

Time is a key in tennis. Create more for yourself. Take it away from your opponent. It sure sounds simple, but good luck being successful.

How do you give yourself a bit more time and steal it from your opponent? Move quickly to the ball. Have your racket in the right hitting position as early as possible. Catch the ball on the rise when possible. Finish your shots aggressively. And reset ASAP! Hit it. Hunt it down. Hit it again! And as always, "grip it and rip it" is a great attitude to have… if it goes in.

What to Do With an Awkward Shot

The ball in an awkward spot should be handled differently than any other shot. Try not to do too much with it. Try not to do too little with it. Everybody thinks the high ball can always be hit hard, but most of you would be better off doing a little less. It takes strength and timing to hit that awkward high ball hard. Just block it back deep and set up for the next shot. You'll be more successful.

"Forfeit" a Game on Purpose to Get Back on Track

Have you ever just gotten off track in a match? You're cruising along and all of a sudden, your game goes away. You get nervous. You get tentative. You panic.

My advice is to forfeit a game on purpose if you need to. (Well, not actually.) But change your attitude to just that thought. Most players start pushing the ball in when they go off the rails. They aim to the middle of the court and become way too safe. This is a bad approach. I say go the other way.

Hit extra hard with extra spin. Exaggerate your follow-through. Go closer to the lines. Be more aggressive! These things actually make you feel better. Attitude can relax you if you are positive. Going for a shot releases tension. Extra spin and follow-through loosen up a tight body. Swinging harder gets rid of frustration. Attempting to "forfeit" a game in this way might actually win you one.

It's just a mental game you're playing with yourself, but you may be amazed at how your body and mind react to this freedom. I wouldn't make a habit of going off-rhythm, but try this sometime and see how it works for you. You're probably going to lose anyway if you can't get your game back on track. But it's way more fun to go down swinging!

Overheads

With the overhead, you should try to hit the pyramids. They're just inside the service box on either side, toward the alley. In amateur tennis, and even at the top levels, it's sometimes more about placement than it is power. Direction on the overhead is the first thought you should have. It's hard to blast it through anybody. I see 90-year-olds that can block it back if you hit it right to them. Nothing against 90-year-olds of course!

Shield Your Eyes on Overheads

Players are commonly taught to point at the ball with their free hand while they set up for an overhead. I have another use for that hand. When the sun is in your eyes, simply spread out all your fingers and shield your vision so you can see the ball better. It feels the same as pointing at the ball, and you'll be better prepared for your smash!

Make Them Hit an Overhead

One of the weakest shots in amateur tennis is the overhead. That's why I coach players at the lower levels to *never* hit a lob out. Don't even flirt with the baseline. Even a short lob can be missed. Players hate waiting on it to come down. The wind plays with it. The sun plays with it. They nearly always over-swing. They mishit it *a lot*. And it gives you tons of time to get ready for their overhead if there is one.

Just Back 'Em Up!

Lobs are easy, right? All you do is hit the ball up. But a short lob gets you killed most of the time, and a long lob goes out. Your goal in lobbing should be to just back up your opponent. Most players aren't very good if you can push them back to no man's land and keep them moving backward while hitting the overhead. So quit hitting it to the baseline where it goes out or short and getting nailed. Just back 'em up!

Push Lobs

You know that player you always complain about, the one that just pushes the ball back over the net (and you all around the court)? Maybe you should take a page out of their book. You can all benefit from developing a push lob.

Opponents who get too close to the net are really susceptible to a lob. I think a quick, short push lob is harder for them to see coming, and easier for most of you to control. The idea is to just back them up, so a long regular, good-looking swing is just too hard to control. Become a pusher when hitting a lob. It will make your game better and annoy your opponents to death.

Moon Ball It!

I sometimes hit a lob just as high as I can while still getting it in on the opposing side. I am amazed at how effective this is, no matter where the ball lands. Players hit it down the middle back to me. They hit it out. They mishit it. Sometimes they even completely whiff it!

It takes a lot of patience to let the ball come down into a hitting position for an overhead. Some players just don't have it. It takes footwork, too. Even though the ball is hit so high and there is plenty of time to set up, some players just don't move as they should. It takes timing to hit the ball falling out of the sky, and even if you let it bounce, it goes back up high again.

A moon ball sounds like a piece of cake to hit, but it isn't. You need to practice how high you can launch a lob and still get it to go in on the other side. At least you'll have fun, especially watching the reaction from your opponent. And the most fun of all is winning the point.

Say, "I'm Here!" Not, "I Got It!"

This may be a little thing, but if it happens on match point and confuses your doubles partner, you will understand why this is so important. When my partner thinks they need to back me up, I like them to say, "I'm here!" It still gives me the decision to take the shot if I think I can make it or bail and receive needed help.

Let's say I'm going back a couple of steps to hit a winning overhead and I hear, "I got it!" Should I pull up and let my partner take it? *No!* I want to take the shot. But if I hear that, it feels like they doubt me, and that might make me doubt myself. Instead, say, "I'm here!" That means I have the option to take the shot or not. This also gives me more confidence in taking the shot.

Also, watch out for confusion between "I got it" and "Got it." "Got it" sometimes sounds like "Got it?" Notice the question mark. It's easy terminology, but saying the right thing to your partner on the court is important.

Strange Lefties

There is just something wrong with a lefty! They hit the ball from the wrong side. They hit this terrible spin so you never know where the ball is going. (I don't really think *they* know where it is going, either.) They construct points almost backward. They just do things differently.

It is still a right-handed world, but on the tennis court the lefty has an unfair advantage. You righties really need to notice the spin and the direction of the bounce when a lefty is hitting. Serving is another baffling shot—with the server even standing facing the wrong way before starting. And that spin keeps coming right into your body.

Here is my expert advice: Pretend to be friends with a left-handed player, and go out and hit and play practice matches with them to figure out some things. But remember in the end that these people are just wrong. They don't do anything normal.

You're Standing in the Wrong Place

L et's say you just hit a shot from anywhere in the court. I'll bet you are *now* standing in the wrong place. After every shot, the court position you need to be in changes. It may be slight, but I always move after every shot. Some change in position may even distract your opponent. You might get lucky and move into the spot the ball is being hit into. You might eliminate an angle that your opponent thought was open. Standing in the same spot is *not* an option. Move!

Squat, Don't Bend

As a good southerner, I try to encourage players to squat as they hit the ball. When you bend the hips, you get into a funny hitting position, and your swing plane changes. Squatting seems to make you drop straight down, bending only at your knees and remaining in good posture to hit the ball.

Simply drop your rear, keep your shoulders square to the ground and lean slightly forward into the shot. This gives you balance and enables you to absorb balls coming at you with pace. I understand that some of you non-southerners may have a problem with this concept because I have tried to explain it to you before, but you really should try it.

Set Up in a Good Ready Position

Have you ever tried to hit a shot from a non-ready position? You have. I've seen you try, and it was not pretty. Think of every shot as a cycle. It begins in a good ready position (remember to squat), and ends in that same exact position, ready for the next shot. You all hit good shots. Some are even great. But then you admire them way too long. When the ball comes back, you are not ready. You need to always set up in a good ready position.

File this little reminder away, too. If you hit it really hard to the other side, you should get back to ready even quicker. If the ball does come back, it will come back faster than you think. "Hit and get set" should be something you say to yourself all the time until it becomes a habit. The only way to get better is to get the next ball back, and the next, and the next, etc., etc. Get my point?

Learn to Dance

Movement on the court is so important. If you move poorly, you have almost no chance of victory. I think you should learn to dance, or at least think of your footwork as a dance. Teach yourself to move smoothly and with rhythm. Teach yourself patterns in your footwork that you can repeat, like a dance step. Teach yourself to flow from shot to shot, like a dance move. Practice your footwork like you would if you were learning a new dance. Smile and have fun like you would if you were dancing. It will help you relax and perform better. You can even try music when you are practicing and see if it helps your rhythm. Movement is learned, much like a dance.

Walk to the Net, Don't Run

I laugh when I see a player running to the net, only to have the ball fly right past them. You have to stop, or at least pause, in order to make an effective change in direction. Split-step? Anybody heard of that?

Try walking to the net so you can make a split-step. At the very least, slow down. At most levels, you don't really need to sprint to the net anyway. Work your way into the net position rather than bolting in and having the ball zip past you. Forward movement in any form is good if you control the point. Learn to make volleys from everywhere on the court, and just keep on walking to the net.

Volley Position

Nearly all players stand too close to the net to volley. It is great to be close if someone will hit it right to you, but they never do in a match. They go around you, over you, or through you. The ideal volley position is one step inside the service line. You can step in to volley better from here. You can defend yourself on balls hit hard because you have a little more response time. You can also cover more lobs on your side of the court without yelling "Yours!" and crossing to the other side.

I like to teach players to volley with their legs and feet. Step into a volley instead of swatting at it with your arms. Your body weight is then behind the shot and your volley is more forceful. Just remember to move back so you are not too close to the net and in harm's way… again!

The Statue of Liberty

Everyone has a picture of Lady Liberty in their minds, right? Maybe that is why you don't turn your shoulders or your body when volleying. Instead, you just stick your arm up in the air! The ball then goes straight into the bottom of the net because the only way you can swing from the Statue of Liberty position is down. It is a patriotic miss, and that's pretty much the only good thing I can say about it.

Return Balls Hit at You at the Net as a Backhand

A ball coming straight at you when you are positioned at the net should always be a backhand. Your backhand is on the front side of your body as you turn your shoulders. This enables you to make contact out in front of your body instead of getting jammed. You really only need to use your opponent's pace anyway to direct the volley to an open spot on the court. If you choose forehand and don't have a lot of time, you'll never get the racket back out in front to a hitting position. Late in this case loses!

Weakest Shot in Tennis

The weakest shot in tennis for everyone (except Federer) is the high backhand volley. Most always, there is something you can do about it. Like not hit it. If you can recognize it early enough, you almost always have time to do a 180 and sidestep the shot to hit a forehand or maybe even a regular overhead. Think quickly and move quickly the next time you get a high backhand volley. If you don't get around to the other side, you're probably hitting a weak shot and likely losing the point.

Between-the-Legs Volley

This is a last-ditch effort and a shot you can use to show off in front of your friends. A ball is coming straight at you, low enough to go between your legs but not hit you in a bad spot. Simply put the racket head on your backside facing forward, tilted very slightly upwards and then drop it right between your legs. No follow-through is recommended! A smile is very helpful to the shot and should have a negative effect on your opponent. Have fun! (And be careful.)

Behind-the-Back Volley

I have to tell you first how I found this shot. In a quick exchange at the net, I was leaning way too far right, and my opponent hit the ball hard to my left side. With the racket also way too far on my right side, I took an upward strike behind me somewhere near my rear end and hit a winning topspin volley. I, of course, shouted, "Yeah, baby!" like I meant to do it. It blew my opponent's mind.

Try a behind-the-back volley just for fun. Turn your body to the right (assuming you're a righty), and simply raise the racket up from low to high with your racket head somewhere near your left cheek. You need a quick, choppy strike, really just almost a wrist flick upward. Good luck!

Left Ear Slap Shot

Your opponent lobbed the ball over your head, but you're going to catch up with it on a really high bounce. Try to position the contact of the ball slightly above your left ear (for righties). Swipe your hand across the front of your face, without hitting yourself, and add a wrist snap like you would use on a spin serve. The intent is to create a side spin with a lot of wrist snap to carry the ball back to the other side. The spin should allow you time to recover and give your opponent another thing to contend with. Just don't hurt yourself.

Never Go Backward

Tennis is a game played best with only forward movement. At worst, I might take a step or two back for an adjustment on a ball, but even then I realize I am giving up valuable territory. Learn to catch the ball on the rise or even to step forward and take the ball out of the air. Both options are better than giving up ground.

And what about a lob? You have to go backward, right? Wrong! Turn first, and analyze how far you need to go to get under the lob. Then turn "backward into forward" by running toward the baseline, looking over your shoulder until you get in the hitting position. Now you can smash away. Always think forward or attack, and quit getting pushed back.

Brace Yourself

I'm going to hit you a hard, deep drive, and I don't want to see you get pushed back. Good luck! This is an important shot to practice. You simply cannot allow opponents to push you way behind the base-line. It's ground you may never recover. So brace yourself, shorten your backswing, keep your shoulders square, lean into the ball, and follow through. Attempt to keep the ball low and drive it as deep as you can.

Where Is Too Far Back?

How fast are you? Are you fast or quick? Are you both? These are really good questions to ask yourself daily. Things change from day to day, and as we age, they especially change. When I was younger, I was both fast and quick. My first step was explosive toward the ball. My speed started immediately, and I could maintain it for a long period of time. I could run down balls if I had to, and I could cut balls while moving forward if I needed to.

If you are quick, you should play closer in. Catch the ball on the rise and even move forward to volley the ball before it bounces. If you are fast, you can play well behind the baseline, which allows you to run down shots and have more time to swing out at the ball. You can still run forward to cover the short balls as well.

And what if you feel like you're neither quick nor fast? Age obviously has an impact on speed. Yesterday and last night do as well. Did you run ten miles yesterday? Did you have a late night last night? Life affects how you feel on the court. Learn what the feeling of the day is for your body. I think about it as I start any match or hitting session, and it helps me to better formulate a plan and strategy

The Point of No Return: Where Is It?

I have this discussion daily. Where is too close to the net? My rule of thumb: Play no closer in than you can cover behind yourself.

When I was young, I could play really close to the net and put the ball away with ease. I also had the speed to cover most lobs. And I had hands quick enough to handle the blast that was coming right at me. But as I have aged and slowed down, I have found way more success when I play further back. I can still step into the volley. I can also cover more lobs. And I have bought myself a fraction more time for the ball coming right at me.

That really short ball that is dropping just over the net is not always a good thing. You should have two thoughts on your way to that shot. First, "Put it away!" And second, "Back up fast just in case I didn't put it away!" Every player has a point on the court that is just too close. Find out where your point of no return is.

Learn to Tolerate No Man's Land

I argue this point at least once a week. I love the pros who tell you to stay out of no man's land, the area between the baseline and the service line. I say good luck!

I believe you should actually practice a lot from no man's land. It is impossible to avoid, and you are going to get caught there no matter how hard you try not to. I'm not telling you to stay there in a match, but in your practice sessions you need to spend a good amount of time in no man's land to get better there. Half-volleys, half-ground strokes, and awkward shots all seem to be the norm in no man's land, and you need to learn to manufacture some kind of decent shot. I know very few people who are really great from this area of the court, but I know that learning to tolerate it will improve your game.

I Knew You Were Going to Do That!

Then why didn't you do something about it? It's crazy to not act on your court instincts. The longer you play, the more you sense certain shots. And I agree that you sometimes know what the next shot will be. What I don't understand is why you do nothing about it.

I learned a long time ago to act on my instincts—anticipate shots and then head them off. If you think your opponent is going to hit somewhere, move there. You may cover the shot. You may distract your opponent. You may make them change their mind and miss. And at the very least, you can quit saying, "I knew you were going to do that!"

No Gold in the Alley

I love to see my doubles opponents guarding the alley. It gives me much more room up the center of the court, over the lower part of the net. There is no gold in the alley. Quit guarding it like there is. In fact, guard the center, and give up some of the alley. Make your opponent hit over the high part of the net next to the outside line.

Play Singles
for Better Doubles

Over-cover the singles court when you are play-ing doubles to win more matches. Squeeze the center with your doubles partner and make your opponents aim more to the alley, where the net is higher and out of bounds comes into play.

Take a look at the marks on the court after you play your next match. The alleys have some, but look at all the play in the singles court. Way more. Remember that the alley is hard to hit over and over again. Give it up a little and see if your opponents are good enough to hit it there consistently. If they do, you probably just lost to a really good team. Or they have gotten lucky. I'd challenge them to a rematch.

Move with Your Partner

A doubles team is a unit. You need to learn to move together with your partner. It is impossible to cover the whole court at all times, but you can cover most of it if you move in the same direction as your partner most of the time. Staying together is especially needed with lateral shots. If my partner moves right three steps, so do I. If my partner is pushed left four steps, I move over about the same to cover behind him.

Of course, there are always exceptions. For example, if my partner closes in to cover a drop shot, I probably need to move back slightly to cover the upcoming lob. If my partner has to go way back for a lob, I probably move forward a little to cover anything short.

The majority of the time, if your partner moves right, you move right to cover the center of the court. Leave the hardest shot more open and tease your opponent into trying it. If they make it over and over, you will have to adjust. But make them hit it more than once. Most opponents can't.

Looking for Something to Do at the Net?

Have you ever been playing doubles and you're standing at the net watching the ball go cross-court over and over between your partner and an opponent? Sure, you have. Well, then why not do something about it? For example, you can cross and really have some fun with that ball. When your partner serves down the middle, it's fun to tear out across there and put the ball away. It will get in your opponent's head. And the worst thing that can happen is you look stupid and blow the point. So what? One point will probably not make you lose. And besides being fun, it can really upset an opponent. That, too, can be fun.

What Is a V Pattern?

In singles, either a V pattern or an upside down V pattern exists. It's created when I hit balls to my opponent down the middle, and I have to run more from side to side to get to his shots. That makes me steer the ball back to the middle, which only continues the vicious cycle. Now, the opposite occurs when I hit the ball to the sides against my opponent. More balls are hit back to the middle on my side, and I can keep my opponent on the run. (I love this outcome.)

The hard thing to do is break the V pattern while in play. If you start to get pulled from side to side, you must really fight the urge to send the ball safely back to the other side down the middle of the court. Instead, try to hit a sharp angled shot or a ball up the line, and see if you can get your opponent to send the ball back to the middle on your side. Opponents on the run miss more shots than opponents standing in the middle of the court.

Why Your Serve Is So Bad

FBI! (And I'm not talking about the Federal Bureau of Investigation.) The worst thing that ever happened to the serve is "first ball in." But you never practice your serve, so it's no wonder it is so bad. Get some help form a pro or a friend to refine it.

There are so many moving parts in a serve. But I see all sorts of motions that are successful. Does Rafa serve like Roger? No, yet each has a great serve. Repetition is the key. A bad toss is usually the cause of a bad serve. If your toss is all over the sky, how do you expect to develop a good motion? If you put the toss in a good position consistently, your serve will improve greatly.

The serve motion is complicated. Everyone is different, so I don't teach just one motion. But you have to put in the time. You'll be amazed what five minutes every other day will do for your serve. Get a good toss. Get a good motion for you. You'll have a better serve.

Place vs. Toss

I've always thought of the toss on my serve as a placement. Toss infers I sling the ball into the air. I want more control, so I think of simply placing the ball in the spot where I want to contact it. You don't have to swing at every ball you toss in the air. Rather, try to place the ball in a better spot and see if your serve doesn't improve.

At What Angle Is the Perfect Serve Hit?

This is a funny tale. I worked at a tennis club for years in Huntsville, Alabama. A lot of really smart engineers lived in our city. One day a gentleman walked onto my court to work on his serve. Before hitting a ball, he asked, "What angle is a perfect serve hit at?" I didn't know the answer, but without hesitation I said, "Approximately 56 degrees." He looked at me, thought for a moment, and replied, "That makes sense."

To this day, I don't know the proper angle for a serve. I do know that it varies with height, ball toss, and spin among other things. On that day long ago, my client needed a starting point, and I gave him one. My goal was to get him to toss the ball out in front so he would be hitting down on it. We worked on the ball toss exclusively for 15 minutes until he decided it was being placed at the proper spot. His toss and serve got better in that session. He had something to work with, and he was plenty smart enough to tweak it as needed. Success comes from repetition, and I saw him get better with practice. He figured out the proper angle for his serve all on his own.

Hit 10 Serves in a Row in the Box... Every Day

'll bet I can improve your serve with this simple piece of advice: Hit 10 serves a day in a row in the proper box. That's it. In order to do this, your motion slows down and you get more consistent. You learn to concentrate better and handle the pressure of the second serve. In the process, your first serve improves without actually trying. Consistency breeds confidence. If you know you can get your second serve in, it will free up the mind so that the first serve becomes more dangerous. At first, it might take you some time to get 10 in consecutively. Don't cheat yourself. Make yourself do it. In a month, you will notice a huge difference.

Serve & Volley, but Serve Slower

Let's say I hit a great, superfast serve and the returner miraculously blocks it back toward me as I am coming into the net. I've just cut my own reaction time down. Try taking a little pace off the serve if you are coming in behind it. That will allow you time to advance into a better net position and set your feet on your split-step. You can also add some spin to the serve to give the returner something besides pace to deal with. There's no reason to try to hit a winner. Place your serve well, and if it turns out to be a winner, great. Let your opponent miss some shots and get frustrated. It can only help in the long run.

Serve with a Twist

I t is actually hard to hit a serve without some spin on it. You have to have the racket moving straight through the ball with no rotation from your wrist to the right or left. It's tough to do, but it will be a speedy serve if you can pull it off.

Spin adds another dimension to the serve. Most righties add a little side spin at contact by snapping the wrist to the right. It's just a more natural finish for most. But depending on the grip, I have seen the wrist snap go in the complete opposite direction, creating the complete opposite spin. Either can be very effective.

The lesson here is to add a little twist to your serve. Serve with different grips and wrist snaps to see what spin you can put on the ball. Think of these changes as additions to your regular serve. Be careful not to strain or hurt your wrist. Different snap directions and grips use different muscles. Every change you make will need a lot of tweaking.

Vary Your Serve Position to Create Return Issues

Do you serve from the same position every time? (You don't have to answer that because I know you do.) Most tennis players are creatures of habit. They do the same thing over and over. They've practiced specific moves, so it's to be expected. But what if you were smart enough to actually create havoc before the point begins?

Let's say you stand right by the center line to serve every time. Now it's 30–40, and you slide out to the singles sideline to begin you serve. Before any toss even occurs, you have created a new issue for the returner. Are you going wide? Should they move over? Is this serve going to be kicked out wide? The doubt you have created just by moving your starting serve position will play to your advantage.

You can also set up your strengths better by standing in various positions. If you don't mind an extra step or two, leave an opening or the appearance of one showing for your opponent to look at. Most of the time they can't resist. They often over-hit the return, and sometimes miss it altogether.

And learn to be creative. Standing wide means I'm going wide, right? Not necessarily. Practice hitting serves from up and down the baseline and to all spots in the opposing service boxes. The ability to have your opponent guessing on where the serve is coming from and going is invaluable.

I Know Where You Are Serving

Well, sort of. I want you to think of your opponent's serve like I do. First, remember that it's a short ball. I know which quadrant of the court it is going to land in. And I get to set up right behind that area of the court before they even hit the serve. Wow. I got this!

Have a forehand in mind and a backhand in mind, and if they hit it right where you have imagined it, crank it! If they miss their first serve, move up a step, smile at them and really be aggressive with the return. That smile, by the way, relaxes you and makes them mad.

Mix it up. Aggressive does not always mean hit it hard. Hit a drop shot. Hit a lob. Cut it cross-court. Roll it cross-court. Drive it down the line. They won't know what hit them, and that puts enormous pressure on their serve. You might even cause them to double-fault, another great way to get them frustrated. Sure, they will sometimes hit a good serve that you haven't imagined. But if you will think like I do, it won't happen often.

Where Should You Stand When You Receive Serve?

The simple answer is anywhere you want. You should absolutely move all over the place. Step to one side to set up your big forehand. Step to the other side to set up a slice backhand. Move back a few steps to get more time for a bigger swing. Move up and half-volley the return and rush the net. (Some call this the "saber." I did it in college about a hundred years ago, but it had no name back then.) The point is to mix things up. Give your opponent a different look, especially if they hit the same serve often. Use your return as an opportunity to get the jump on them and do something different.

Play Pretty

I am a huge Roger Federer fan. His grace and technique on the court are pretty to watch. We should all follow his lead. You will play longer for sure and probably better, too. Sometimes you see Federer hit shots off his back foot or from an unbalanced position that his opponent has put him in, but not often. Good technique will keep you from getting injured. It will make you more consistent. It certainly makes you look better.

I want you playing tennis the rest of your life. Roger has been relatively healthy most of his long career. I believe his longevity comes from being pretty on the court. Crazy grips are hard on your arms. Crazy stances are hard on your back. Crazy motions are hard on your whole body. Work on being consistent with good technique and only manufacture shots when you have to. Stay healthy and play pretty for the rest of your life.

Balance

This may be the most important thing I talk about in this book. Balance is vital in almost every sport. Tennis is no different. Some form of balance is required for any shot. I'm amazed watching pro players jump into the air to make a shot, but even more amazed at the balance they still possess. Most of you don't have that. Trust me. I see you jump, and it is not a pretty sight.

The next time you go out and hit, try doing one rally with just power. Blast it as hard as you can. Next rally, hit it as hard as you can while maintaining enough balance to make the shot. I know which one will be more consistent. Hit as hard as you can with balance. If your body is out of control, so is the shot.

"You Messed Up and Did It Right!"

When I was very young, my dad often said this very thing to me. It was always followed by, "If you can do it right once, then you can do it over and over." I came to live by these words on the court. I can remember hitting a winner by accident and thinking to myself, "Repeat that." My dad's philosophy may have been a different sort of teaching tool, but for me it was very effective. I learned to think on the court and notice what worked and what didn't.

Turn, Turn, Turn

Sounds like an old song, doesn't it? It is also a good teaching technique that we pros use. I know if I can get you to turn away from the incoming ball, you will turn back through the shot as the ball goes back to the other side, and then you will turn once more to reset. Turning provides you with more power. It puts your body weight behind your shots, and helps disguise them. In addition, opponents don't know exactly how much you are going to come out of your turn and direct the ball. At upper levels of tennis, being deceptive with your shot placement is paramount. And, of course, we know how important power has become in today's modern game.

Slow Down

My dad had a great saying, "You couldn't wait to miss that shot, son!" He was right. And you all do it. Tennis shots need to develop. If you can slow yourself down, it will help you make your shots. You still need to prepare early. Pick your shot. Commit to it so you can get ready. Get your racket back or in the proper spot for the chosen shot. Then it's time to execute, but at the appropriate speed. If you rush, you'll likely miss.

Moving to the ball is obviously crucial. But getting to the ball too early can also be bad. Most of you have the patience of a rabbit, and you also jump around like one. Taking time to step into a shot or through a volley with balance will aid in your ability to make more shots.

I like my last step into a shot to be aggressive so I have my body weight behind it. I may actually slow up in the middle on my way to the shot. That way I can make my last step aggressively. Getting there too early can make you pull off of a shot or even change your commitment to it. Both are bad things.

Finally, finish your shot. Once you choose the shot and execute it, make sure you follow through properly and have a full finish. Then return to the ready position. Shuffle back or move to the right spot for the next shot. Slow down to prepare for what's next.

Good Miss!

There really is no such thing as a good miss. But there are times on the court nonetheless when I say it. For example, it's a good miss if you have made a good swing at the ball, and it is going in the right direction in order to win you the point, and then it just clips the top of the net and falls back onto your side. You were inches away from greatness. You probably scared your opponent to death. I don't want to ever hit the ball into the net, but when it is that close, I know I am on the right track.

A Good Shot Hit to the Wrong Place Is Not a Good Shot

Hit the ball away from your opponent. A good shot right at someone is probably going to come back. We have all won a point with a terrible mishit that goes to the right spot. You can't count on those, so think about where you are aiming the ball before you hit and make a better decision. Good shots to bad places are not good shots. They may even come back quicker.

Same Length Swing

We have all had that occasion where we overswing at the ball. Even if the shot goes in (which it usually doesn't), it has less pace than a normal swing would. It's because you don't hit it as solid. Let the weapon in your hand do its job.

Try this sometime in your practice session to help your rhythm. Keep your swing length the same or as near the same as possible. Take the racket back to the same spot and follow through to the same spot. Keep the swing the same length and speed, and concentrate on solid contact. I am not saying that from time to time you can't have more takeaway and/or more follow-through. But try to keep the swing repeatable and see if you don't hit more solid shots.

Backswing

Who has missed that easy volley or sitter by over-swinging? I hope you all raised your hand. I have seen you all do it. Try this: Hit a ball at someone at 100 mph. If they can get the racket pointed in the right direction with the proper angle and make contact in the center of the racket, they will win the point.

You can hit a ball back to an opponent using their pace against them. Shorter backswings enable you to do this. Big backswings are more difficult to control and make it harder to keep your balance. It takes practice to shorten up a backswing, but as you are mastering it, you'll hit it harder because your contact will improve.

Follow-Through or Takeaway?

Which is more important? I think you need both, but sometimes the ball is blasted at you so fast that you don't have time for a proper takeaway. So if I have to choose one, I'd go with follow-through.

If I turn my upper body properly, the racket is already somewhat in a good starting position. When I can get my racket moving forward through a hard-hit shot, then I can make good contact and produce an effective shot with just a follow-through. If I decide on a big takeaway on that same shot, I may not even get back to a hitting position before the ball speeds by me. A good follow-through creates spin and direction. Sometimes it is even responsible for making a shot of sorts when there is no time for one.

The Myth of "Watch the Ball"

I don't believe you should just watch the ball. I teach you to watch your opponent hit the ball. The way someone swings at the ball tells you a lot about what you have to do to get to the ball and hit it back. I always pick the ball up off my opponent's racket, but by watching what they have done to it, I am better prepared to combat the incoming shot.

Listen to the Ball

Do you know why the pros want quiet on the court? We want to hear the ball. There is a huge difference when an opponent strokes the ball solidly versus spinning a shot at me. Sometimes the swings actually look a lot alike. A ball with extreme spin may be hit with a really long, fast swing—the same way you blast a shot. But the sound is different.

Different amounts of spin sound different. Different speeds sound different. Get ready to move up or back on the ball depending on the spin. You absolutely hear when a ball is smashed with excessive power. Shorten your backswing and get ready quickly. Conversely, you know when you don't hear anything at contact that the ball is traveling softly through the air. Run! It is probably a drop shot. Learn to listen as you watch your opponent hit the ball and see if you, too, can tell what is actually coming over the net at you.

And listen to mishits as well. They sound clunky and react strangely because of the imperfect contact. Good luck on figuring out what the ball is going to do, but at least by hearing it, you know something different is coming.

Do You Really See Contact?

Y ou have all heard it, Basic Tennis 101: "Watch the ball." But do you actually see contact? When I am on the dead run chasing a wide forehand and I decide to rip it up the line, believe me, I am trying to watch the ball as closely as I can. But I can't absolutely tell you I see the ball hit the strings as I swing through it.

Through practice and repetition, we develop skills that help us project where the ball is going to be at a certain point in space as we swing at it. I watch the super slow-motion replays of the pros swinging though the ball, and it looks like the top players in the world see the ball just before contact. But then they swing so hard that I'm not sure they see the ball and strings come together.

We call it timing and we all have it, good or bad. Repetition makes you better and more consistent at making contact. And I am not telling you to *not* watch the ball. Please keep looking for it. You will see it on some slow shots for sure.

What Do You See When You Look at the Ball?

I hope you see a lot of things besides the ball. For example, if you look closely, you can sometimes see the rotation or lack of rotation. Hopefully you also see how the ball is struck. If the follow-through was high, the shot probably has topspin. If the follow-through was low, it probably has backspin.

Out of the corner of your eye, can you also see where your opponent is? Do you see any open court anywhere? It takes some practice, but while looking directly at the ball, you should notice these other things. Learn to take advantage of everything you see. Just watching the ball alone probably won't do you much good.

Aim Out

You need to expand where you hit the ball on the court. So at least in practice, and under some pressure situations, aim out! Most people err to the inside and don't actually use the entire court. They don't stretch their opponents to the full extent. In practice, when it doesn't actually cost you a point, aim to the outside of the line. I'll bet you can't hit it out. The mind seems to have a safety valve, and we all tend to miss to the inside. Under pressure, pick a target a little outside the line. You tend to steer it to the inside when you're tight. Figure out how your mind and body work under pressure.

Quit Hitting It Out

Tennis is like everything else in the world—for every piece of advice or instruction, there is a flip side or an exception. I know I told you to aim out, which I believe to be absolutely true at times. Now I'm telling you to *quit* hitting it out. These are only slightly different pieces of instruction.

I have had some opponents who would self-destruct if I could just get another ball back in play. You never know which ball it is that they are going to miss, so most of the time you have to apply at least some pressure. A harder hit ball may do it. A ball slightly farther away from them may win you the point. A shot with little or no pace may be the ball they don't like. At some point, you will realize you have to quit hitting it out. Otherwise, you are the player who is self-destructing.

Find Out Where Out Is

When I take my first five or six swings every day, I try to find out where out is. I suggest you do the same if you ever want to get any better at expanding the court. I cannot believe how safe some players hit it. Sure, the ball goes in, but near the middle of the court nearly every time!

Your first swings are always tight. Aim past the baseline and see if you can even hit it out. Remember that under pressure, you tighten up. These are mental tricks to learn to deal with your own fears and abilities. It is also more fun to find out where out is. It allows you to hit the ball beyond the baseline and wide over the sidelines. It's always easier to play safe, but what fun is that? Be risky and hit the lines. Loosen up and take a chance. You just might get better.

Hit the Imaginary Lines

Do you ever see things that aren't actually there? Good, me, too. I see imaginary lines a couple of feet inside the singles lines when I play, and those become my target. I don't think many people are good enough to aim at the real lines and hit them with any consistency, especially on a big point when it matters the most.

I aim at imaginary lines just inside the real ones. If I miss a little outside that imaginary line, I have some room to play with. If I miss to the inside, my shot will certainly be in, but it just won't stretch my opponent out as much as I had intended. In doubles I can actually use the singles sideline as an aiming point. Or if you're up against really good, quick players, at least aim a little outside the singles sideline. Give yourself some margin for error and see if it helps you.

Aim at the White Part

W ait, didn't you just tell me to not aim at the lines? Well, there are good lines and bad lines. Here is the big benefit you get from hitting any line: confusion. Most hard court lines are pretty consistent bounce-wise when the ball hits them, but some are more slippery than others. Soft court lines are absolutely slippery and often not exactly even with the playing surface. And the ball itself seems to disappear for a split-second when it comes off them.

All these factors are a source of confusion for your opponent, at least for a moment. In doubles, hit the T and watch how that baffles the other team. Hit the back of the service line with a first serve and revel in the outcome. You'll see that some lines are meant to be aimed at.

Soften Your Grip

This tip is tough for most. The analogy I've always heard is grip the racket like it's a bird. You don't want to let it go, but you don't want to strangle it either. Grip pressure is key to every shot. Sure, you need a firm grip sometimes, but you can absolutely wear your arm out if you're squeezing the racket too tightly. You can even cause injury. To develop touch and finesse in your game, you must have a softer grip. It is almost impossible to have maximum grip pressure and create feel in any shot. Try softening your grip next time you practice and see the improvement.

"Funky" Grips

I see what I call "funky" grips all the time. But what I've learned from my teaching is that no two individuals are the same. In other words, funky grips aren't always wrong. My concerns? One, and the most important, is it safe? And two, is it productive? I want everyone to be able to pull off the shot they choose, and for that shot you need a specific grip. But I don't want it to be so funky that it may hurt you in the future due to overuse or repetition. And if your funky grip isn't productive, then I'd try a new one.

47 Forehand Grips

I love it when someone asks me what my forehand grip looks like. I kiddingly reply, "Which of the 47 grips are you talking about?" I can't even tell you how many grips I have. I'll bet more than you think.

A multitude of factors determine the grip you need. Where are you standing on the court? What spin are you hitting? How hard are you going to hit it? Are you hitting into the wind or is it behind you? Where do you want the ball to land? You get the point.

Don't limit yourself to a specific grip because there is no *one* grip for any shot. You will improve through experimentation and practice. Have some fun with grip changes and watch carefully where the ball goes and how much spin you put on it. I promise you that one day you'll need *that* grip and *that* shot.

Concentrate on Technique

I broke my right wrist years ago while snowboarding. The injury forced me to teach left-handed for a couple of months. My technique was immediately pretty good, but I didn't have much arm strength. Watching the ball closely and hitting the sweet spot became more important. And it kinda looks different when swinging from the "wrong" side. Feel or touch was much more difficult. But since the arm was weaker anyway, I learned I could simply use that weakness as touch. When feeding, I still had to hit to specific spots to get my students to react accordingly. When I tried to play wrong handed, I found I could still somewhat move the ball around. I think a lot of you don't use your mind enough. Think. Move the ball around. Watch the ball closer. Weak or slow shots aren't always bad. Concentrate on technique.

Keep It Low or Add Loft?

How can you push your opponent back? Learn to keep the ball low and also add loft to it. Imagine a window of glass above the net about the length of your racket. Bust it out with pace and see if you can still keep the ball deep beyond the service line. This is one way to push your opponent into the backcourt. It cuts their reaction time down and tends to force more errors.

You can also do the opposite and add loft. The advantage is when your opponent lets the ball bounce, it gives you time to recover and they have to generate pace off a shot that has very little of it. The problem is that this shot can be picked off in doubles or fired back by an incoming player moving to the net in singles.

I think both shots have value. Some players "eat" pace—they like the bounce of a good, deep shot. Some players are good at moving forward and catching the ball on the rise. You need to understand what shot seems to hurt your opponent and use it the most. Work on keeping it low and also on adding loft.

Mishit Winners

Have you ever noticed how hard it is to hit a good shot off an opponent's mishit? It has weird pace and funky spin. It's impossible to read and doesn't go where it was intended. When you see and hear a mishit happen, I suggest the use of some restraint. Just because your opponent shanked one does not mean you are going to have an easy shot. In fact, it's probably just the opposite.

Seeing Is Believing

I'll never forget the first day of college tennis when the coaches filmed us. We all thought we were hot-shots coming right out of high school. The videos we saw the next day told a bit of a different story. Get someone to take video of you on the court. You won't believe how you look hitting a ball. Mistakes are not always felt, but you can certainly see them. And it's easier to fix things when you see yourself doing them. Get a pro to show you the right way. You'll have to practice. A lot!

"Righter" and "Lefter"

I like to use memorable terms or phrases when teaching. I'm sure I get this from my dad. I tell my juniors and even some of my adults to aim "righter" or "lefter" on their shots and especially their serves. This fun way of thinking may not be grammatically correct, but it registers with them. Adding direction while keeping things loose will give you better results.

Drill Speed

Drills should be done at different speeds on different days. Actually, you should probably change up the drill speed during the same day as well. Look at it this way. Opponents hit the ball at different speeds, so you should practice the feed at different speeds. I have seen players who could handle a hard shot better than they could a soft shot. And I've seen players who couldn't handle speed at all. A combination of speed, touch, and placement may be your best option.

The Approach Shot Drill

The drill I start with most days is the approach shot drill. I simply feed you a short ball to encourage you to keep it low, hit it hard to the appropriate spot on the court, and follow it to the net. In doubles in particular, the transition from the baseline to the net position is very important, and we don't practice it nearly enough.

Learn from the Fence Line

In my clinics with as many as eight people on a court at a time, it is important to use non-playing time wisely. When you are standing at the fence line, watch the point in front of you. Notice how the point develops. Do the players do things differently than you do? Of course, they do. There are a lot of ways to win a point. You can learn from everyone on the court, not just the pro.

The Nasty Ball

The nasty ball is both a drill and a shot. The drill starts by feeding a floater that would land in no man's land. You have to volley the ball out of the air. In competitive play, I see this shot hurt people so badly. It's an awkward ball that doesn't have pace. You can hit it with a flat volley, or go for the aggressive swinging topspin volley.

Repeat, Repeat

Tennis is a funny game. You need to do things over and over. The drills I'm encouraging you to do aren't new. Different pros call these drills different things, but hopefully you've done them all before. If not, you need a new pro!

When you're doing the drills, practice hitting to a specific spot. Remember when you're playing a match to "flip the switch" and hit it away from your opponent. The one place you don't want to hit it is right to someone.

With today's racket technology and the "weapons" everyone has in hand, the ball will come back if you hit it right to somebody, almost guaranteed. Be spot specific and make sure that spot is away from your opponent, making them work harder.

The Alley Rally

We did these great practice rallies in college called "Alley Rally." You simply stand behind the alley on your side and your partner stands on the other side of the court across from you. Then you rally into the alley as consistently as you can. Try this with multiple alleys, not just the ones you can see. Put down balls to make your own practice alleys. Change them up as many ways as you can imagine and really work on targeting different shots. Then put it into your play and see how you've improved your control and consistency.

The 6-Ball Drill

My favorite drill is one I hope you've done over and over: the six-ball drill. You get a forehand, a backhand, an approach shot, forehand volley, backhand volley and an overhead. The transition from shot to shot should be practiced over and over to smooth them out.

Volley Drill

Set up close to the net on opposite sides with your partner. Try to volley the ball right to your partner and have them do the same right back to you. Be as consistent as you can. Then back up and do the same drill with only forehands. Next try with only backhands. The main thing is that you keep the ball going to increase your consistency and reflexes.

Footwork Drill

A really simple but effective footwork drill is side vs. side. Put three to six players on each side of the net at the baseline in a single file line. Feed the ball to one side, and the first player hits ball to other side trying to win the point. The point is played inside the singles lines. But instead of watching and admiring the shot like normal, the player that just hit the shot goes to the end of the line and the next player up plays the incoming shot. You've got to move! Play to eleven, then switch sides and feed the other team.

An advanced strategy for this drill/game is to hit it at the player that just hit the ball. If the player hasn't done a good job of moving right after making the shot, then he or she is in the way of the incoming partner. Hit, MOVE, and then watch, instead of hit, WATCH, and then MOVE to catch up.

3-on-2 Drills

Another favorite drill of mine is three-on-two. Two players are at the net in front of a pro. Another two players are on the baseline on the other side. Once the ball is in play, if it gets past the two people at the net, the pro keeps it in play. This helps everybody to stay focused and return balls even when they don't think it's coming back. Never assume you've won the point until the point is completely over. Sometimes your lame partner actually backs you up or comes through somehow!

Pick a Spot

Whether you're doing a drill or you're in play, you should always try to hit to a spot. Don't just mindlessly knock the ball to the other side of the net. That simply does you no good. Pick out a specific spot and concentrate so that you can hit the ball there over and over. And then move the spot. It takes a lot of repetition, but you should be able to hit spots all over the court. A helpful hint: It should be away from your opponent.

The Ball Machine

Have you ever used the ball machine? I think it's pretty boring. That being said, it can be helpful for working on a specific shot, and you can always get a good workout by doing side-by-sides. My advice is to never use it for more than 15 to 20 minutes or you'll go brain-dead.

Patterns Are a Good Start

Your teaching pro does drills with you to develop hitting patterns. I ask my students to hit to a specific spot on the court over and over. That is the beginning of a pattern. When I ask them to do it in conjunction with another shot, then we have a pattern.

Down the lines, cross-courts, deep sets up short, short sets up deep, and so on. These patterns are a good starting point for any match. Notice how your opponent reacts to each pattern and remember which one gives them the most difficulty. Now you have a good game plan or at the least the start to one.

My Warm-Up

Different players require different things out of a warm-up. Times also vary. I've had leagues where the players would want to warm up for an hour before they actually started their match (which seemed excessive). Remember that your real warm-up is actually timed.

I call my personal warm-up "4646." I like to start at the net, really close, where I hit four successful, solid volleys. I move back three steps to my favorite position, just inside the service line, and I hit six solid, well-placed deep volleys. I back up three more steps and hit four decent, relatively solid shots of any sort from no man's land. Then I back up to just behind the baseline and hit six solid ground strokes that I feel are well controlled. It often takes more than just four or six tries to get the desired outcome from all these positions. Then I hit about 10 good second serves and one or two good first serves. That is also my overhead practice. I don't take lobs.

Go Watch Live

Everyone loves to watch a great match on television. You get to hear the comments from the announcers who are ex-players and actually know something about the game. I even like that I can go get a drink and snack on the changeovers while the commercials are airing.

But you should go watch live. The television really slows play down. You cannot believe how fast the players are. Their court coverage is fantastic. You cannot believe how hard they strike they ball. The spin they create is enormous. You cannot believe the work they put forth to win a single point. The angles they hit are unreal. I don't think these things show up on television like they do in person.

Their changeovers are spent doing things to get them ready to get back up and do it all over again. They don't snack like I do during the changeover. They look like they are replacing nutrients in their body. They also look like they are formulating a plan. They check their equipment. They relax. They do so many things you don't see during the commercial break. The downtime of the changeover is valuable to them, and they use it wisely.

Above all, it is electric to be there in the presence of these great athletes. It really does feel like they are special people. It is motivating to me to watch them live, so much more than watching on a screen. Go watch live!

Grunting

I understand that sometimes more effort is used to hit certain shots and sometimes you struggle to make a shot. These situations might require a grunt. But you will never convince me that some of the sounds you hear from the other side are not meant to be a distraction. I think something should be done about grunting, but with high-profile players doing it, I suspect nothing ever will.

3 Challenges

In this day and age of technology, why do pro players only get three challenges to correct bad or missed calls? We don't want to expand the time it takes to play a match, but this is NOT the place to cut time. Chair umpires, please watch the match and overrule bad line calls. Don't just ask if a player wants to challenge the call. Or have shot spot BEEP loudly when the ball is out. We can do away with the linespeople, too. Players today hit the ball so hard that it is hard for the human eye to see. The technology is there. Let's use it and get it right!

Shot Clock

I think we have gotten to the point in tennis where we actually need a shot clock. That's sad. I must say, though, that I understand the value of sometimes slowing down play. I remember a match in college against a player who stalled after every lost point. After I complained to him, he did nothing. Sweet person that I am, I decided to give it right back to him, but with even more time and aggravation. I bounced the ball off my foot. I slowly walked to pick up the balls even slower than he did. I had to tie my shoes multiple times. Guess what? He complained. It took me almost three hours to beat the fool. We could have avoided all the drama with a shot clock.

The top players seem to extend the time on the shot clock. They vigorously complain if they get a warning or a penalty. It is gamesmanship. Period! Who has the time or wants to watch a match for five hours with much of it featuring players bouncing the ball before they serve or toweling off?

Coaching from the Sidelines or Stands

This is a problem at every single level of tennis. Again, it's sad that it's true. Do people read and know the rules? If so, then they simply decide that cheating is okay. Sometimes you just need to call it as it is. I think we could get this fixed with more enforcement. I wish there were a way to embarrass people and coaches who blatantly break the rules of the game. Or we could make coaching legal for everyone, and thus slow the game to a snail's pace. (Just kidding!)

The Greatest of All Time: Things Change

I am a huge Federer fan. I used to be a huge Connors fan. Then I was a huge Borg fan. I had the honor of meeting Arthur Ashe and Rod Laver and loved watching the clips of their matches back in their prime. You could argue that any one of those mentioned (along with countless others) is the greatest of all time. Watching today's game versus play in the past simply reminds you of how things change.

The weapons used by players today are so much better than in the past. Clothing, shoes, and all equipment have come so far. Training and nutrition are a big part of the leaps in today's game, too. Travel itself has improved so much that it has become a factor in the evolution of the game.

I don't think we need to put limits on the progress of tennis. Let players develop in different ways and atmospheres. Experiment with new techniques, and keep trying to advance the game. I remember hearing from someone when Borg came onto the scene, "He will never be great. He is too unorthodox." And look at the styles of Roger versus Rafa. Greatness comes in all sizes, shapes, styles, and techniques. Things change.

Read The Code

The Code is a guide for players by USTA Officiating that outlines "fair play and the unwritten rules of tennis." It goes hand in hand with the International Federation of Tennis Rules of Tennis and outlines procedures all players should follow that make the sport better. Make your junior players read *The Code* when they are old enough to really understand it. Every parent should read and memorize *The Code*. So many things in life would be fixed with a little common sense. All tennis players would benefit from using a little more of it. That's the way I think of *The Code*. Have you actually read it?

Winning Is Easy

I can tell you how to win every match you will ever play. It is so simple you will feel stupid for not thinking of it yourself. You are going to marvel at the wisdom I possess and be shocked that I am passing it on to you. Here goes… Hit the last ball in.

Think about it and notice the smile that creeps across your face. Learn to be consistent enough to always get one more ball back than your opponent and you will win every point and match you ever play. This works at every level. I'm amazed by the pros hitting some of the shots they do. But that last shot that goes in is the one that you need to work on. Consistency wins.

"Play" like Earl & Pearl

We have two pretty famous creatures here at Seaside tennis. Their names are Earl and Pearl. They are squirrels. They play on the fences pretty much all day, and they assist me in my teaching. You might think I am joking, but I'm not. They exhibit a trait I try to get into everyone on the court. Play.

They run along the fences and the trees surrounding the court playing chase and I assume retrieving food. They take short little breaks but then get right back at their mission. Whatever that is. But they seem to enjoy what they are doing though they are clearly working pretty hard at it.

I point this out occasionally to my clients who are all wound up about the shot they missed. Or the student having trouble with their serve. I point out that you can work hard and still enjoy what it is you are working on if you treat it more like fun. Remember, we are supposed to "play" tennis. It is a great, fun game. I have certainly worked hard to improve but I never lost sight of the pure enjoyment I get from hitting a shot perfectly. I think you would all benefit if you would adopt the same drive of Earl and Pearl.

See the Good in the Game

Tennis is just a game. For most of us, that is all it will ever be, and that should be enough. You should all see the good in the game. I know you have heard that if you don't see the ball land out, it is good. I hope that is the way you play the game. I have so much more fun when I can return the ball that has hit the line from my opponent. I have never understood what calling a ball out does for you if you know it was in. Even if it embarrasses you, please admit the mistake and reverse your call. Hopefully that goodwill is then returned from your opponent. And even if it isn't, does it really matter that much to you? I know a close call can change the outcome of a close match, but I think in the long run you will have far more success in the game of tennis if you see the good!

Parting Words of Wisdom

Nearly every tip I've given you has an exception. That's what makes tennis so much fun. Be consistent. But if your opponent is more consistent, then your only chance is to be more offensive and hope you can hold it together long enough to blow them off the court. That's just one of the many examples of the contradictions of tennis. I think the bottom line is to stay loose, have fun, and walk away happy. That will make your decision to improve your game stick. They say you'll never work a day in your life if you do a job you love. I think that's why I got into tennis. It's a great game that I absolutely love!

From the Archives...

For a while now I've been a contributing columnist for the *Seaside Times*. It's a fun role that allows me to offer my opinion on a variety of tennis-related topics. I'd like to share some of my favorite columns with you.

How to Beat the Heat So the Heat Doesn't Beat You

originally published July/August 2013

Preparing for your tennis match is crucial. And I'm not just talking about your strokes. With the high temperatures and humidity we have here at the beach, you have to be prepared so you can beat the heat.

In order to win a match, you have to be there at the end, playing hard and smart, and not melting in the heat like a shave ice on a hot day. How can you accomplish that? Start by hydrating before the match, and keep drinking at every changeover. It doesn't matter if it's water or your favorite sports drink. The trick is to keep the fluids flowing to replace what you're sweating out.

You also need to protect yourself from the sun. Like every outdoor activity here, apply sunscreen liberally before leaving the house. Then wash the sunscreen off your hands so that your grip doesn't slip. If there's no covered seating on the court, you may want to take an umbrella to sit under during breaks. (Hey, the pros on tour do it, although you'll have to find your own ball boy or ball girl to hold it for you.) On almost every court, you're likely to find a small spot of shade, so if your opponents are talking strategy on their side of the court, go to your shady spot until they are ready to start the point.

To help keep your cool on the court, wear performance clothing. The moisture-wicking fabrics of today's performance apparel will make you feel cooler and dryer than your fashion cotton tees. Keep a change of clothing in your tennis bag, and if you feel especially wet, make a change. A dry shirt or socks will go a long way in making you feel instantly refreshed. Make sunglasses, sweatbands, hats, and visors a part of your tennis wardrobe.

Keep a towel handy to wipe away the sweat and dry your hands. Improve your grip on the racket with a rosin bag, tacky towel, or a new overgrip. Some overgrips are designed to absorb sweat, while others have a tacky feel to help you hold on to the racket.

Take a cooler to keep your drinks cold. You can even put a towel on ice to wrap around your neck at changeovers. And always take the fully allotted breaks at changeovers and between points when the temperatures are high.

Lastly, use the serve and volley and the chip and charge to speed up play while on the court. You don't want to rally back and forth from the baseline repeatedly. Shorten your points to help beat the heat.

Let your opponents sweat, and be there at the end to shake hands for the win.

Technology and Your Tennis Game

originally published September/October 2013

Technology has given the sports industry a leap up in speed and power. The trend is evident in every sport, and tennis is no exception. Those who don't change rackets every year or two are likely to miss the ball—literally.

Rackets are now made from titanium or a composite of materials that are more powerful than ever. The days of wood and aluminum are so far past that they seem ancient when you talk about them. Lighter, stronger materials have made it possible to hit the ball at incredible speeds. It has even changed the way we now teach the game. Loopy shots of the past have been replaced by low, penetrating shots that are just above the net as the ball crosses, and yet the ball lands deep in the court. It's great for pushing opponents back. To combat that, we now teach you how to catch the ball on the rise.

String is the equipment that has had the most upgrades. Polyester, gel-filled, textured, and shaped strings are just a few of the new options on the market. Soft strings have been improved for players with arm and wrist injuries. Harder strings have been built for increased power and spin. It really is amazing to see how the different strings respond and the different effects that can now be created on the tennis ball.

Balls are more technologically advanced as well, now made specifically for different court surfaces. The material the ball is made from is so much better than the ball from the past. And with the new QuickStart tennis for 10-and-under players, balls are made softer and flatter for the slower swing speeds of children.

Shoes are also improved from the basic ones of the past. Shoes are made in hard, soft, and cross-training versions. They are lighter in weight than ever before, and they are engineered to be cooler. Today's shoes are made to accommodate any foot or foot problem a player may have.

Now, tennis clothing is even referred to as equipment, due to its high-tech fabrics. It wicks away moisture. It protects you from the sun with special UV blocking. It breathes to keep you cooler. Apparel can also block the wind to keep you warmer and dryer. I would never play these days in a cotton tee shirt like I did in the past. Remember how it would weigh three pounds at the end of a set?

The Seaside Tennis Pro Shop is prepared to elevate your tennis game with an upgrade of your outdated equipment. With cutting-edge technology, as well as the latest in strings, shoes, accessories, and fashion-forward trends, you can certainly get your game on here. And with private and group lessons from friendly pros you will soon know exactly how to use it all to your advantage.

Court Partners

originally published March/April 2014

Tennis is an individual sport, right? "Singles" is usually what we watch on TV, but "doubles" is actually what we play. And although you only see one player against another on TV, they always thank their "team" at post-match press conferences. Tennis is definitely a team sport.

The ladies' teams I coach here in Seaside are instructed on how to move together, cover for one another, cheer for each other, and provide on-court coaching to their partners. Doubles teams that are successful learn to almost think alike. I call it being on the same page, and it is crucial for strong partnerships. In team clinics, players hear tips on how to master these traits. They hear the same tips. They all learn to think alike on the court. This "being on the same page" will help win matches.

I also get the opportunity to coach visiting teams from Atlanta, New Orleans, Dallas, Knoxville, and so on during the spring and fall. I'm told they don't hear some of my tips back home. I'll bet they do. I can explain how to hit the ball down the middle in doubles, and players somehow hear it better from me simply because it is said in a different way than it was said by their home pro. There really is no one way of doing things in tennis. Different pros teach different things and in different ways. That is a good thing. You should always seek coaching that provides various viewpoints. It is to your advantage to choose what will work best for your game and your team.

Every time you play doubles, one of your opponents is

weaker than the other. (Or possibly just having a bad day.) Never get beat by the best player on the court or by an opponent's best shot. Learn to steer the ball toward the weaker player and set your partner up for more offensive shots. If they hit a piercing forehand, then try to hit it to their backhand. Defensive tennis does not work very often these days. And it is no fun. Learn to be aggressive on the court and take control of the play. Move your partner around on the court, so he or she is able to do more with the ball. Encourage your partner to poach from time to time. And watch the confidence rise on your side of the net and erode on the other.

I love to talk about ways to beat opponents on the court. Come to my daily 8 a.m. Eye-Opener Clinic for more tennis tips and teamwork coaching.

How to Volley Like a Champ

originally published May/June 2014

The volley is one of the key shots in the tennis we play today. Doubles matches have taken over league play, and having a good, sound volley is a must if you want to win. But just taking the ball out of the air is not as simple as you might think.

The volley is a demanding shot requiring quick reaction and technical precision. By moving forward on the court and taking the ball out of the air, you put pressure on your opponents and put yourself in an offensive position. At the net, you open up more angles and have more opportunities to hit clean winners.

The traditional volley is taught using a continental grip, holding the racket head up. You lead with the handle while keeping the racket face slightly open. The ball is hit with a very short "punch" stroke through the ball as you move your body forward through the hitting zone. It is the most simple and dependable way to hit a solid volley. The ball being volleyed is usually traveling very rapidly toward you, and a good, strong grip position is needed to absorb the impact.

The game of tennis is changing, and so is the way we hit volleys. The new method is a swinging volley. It is a swing very similar to your topspin ground stroke. It is harder to time, but it can provide more net clearance and certainly more power and spin than the "old" volley. Grip changes are also needed for a forehand versus a backhand volley. And time is a huge factor if the ball coming toward you is moving fast.

These days, you need variety in all aspects of your tennis game, including your volley. The problem with variety though is having time to make a decision, making the "right" decision, and then executing the shot. Good luck!

Get out and work on all versions of the volley and see how you can insert them into your tennis game. Come see us at Seaside Tennis to work out the kinks in this fun but necessary shot. See you on the courts.

How to Watch Tennis on the Tube

originally published July/August 2014

Couch potatoes, you're going to love the tip this month. With all the rain we have received over the last year, I'm going to help you learn by watching a tennis match—on television.

Now that there is a channel dedicated to tennis and all the major tournaments are aired on numerous channels, it's easy to find a good match on TV. Particularly on rainy days when I cannot get the courts playable due to heavy rain, watch a match and learn from the comfort of your own couch.

Look first at the players' court position. Are they on the baseline moving side to side, or are they pressing to get to the net? Singles is primarily played from the baseline these days, while doubles is played by trying to control the net. Watch how players move and recover after each shot. Focus on one player's movement and check out the footwork, court coverage and tactics that they play with. And then see how the opponent tries different things to counteract those tactics.

Listen to the announcers. A lot of the commentators are ex-players and have great insights as to how the game is being played. Former No. 1 players like Courier, McEnroe, Everett, and Navratilova are often heard giving tips and analysis of ongoing matches. How lucky are we to hear what a "real player" is thinking? These players are light-years ahead of us in their on-court thinking and strategy. Try to implement their advice into your own game.

And last, and I think most fun, turn the volume off and really watch the point. Notice how the pros play points, and compare it to how you play points. Note their patience, their depth, their spins, their variety, and their great footwork. Think about some of your past matches and see how these things could have helped you win a close match. And think how fun it will be to try some of these things the next time you play!

You can always learn something from watching a televised match of some of the greatest players on the planet. Or you could come see me and let me pick on you and help you out on the court. Either way, I hope you are always trying to learn something new and fun!

It's All in the Racket

originally published September/October 2014

Want to "buy" a better game? These days you can with the incredible advances in racket technology. Every company makes a great frame, but they all differ slightly in their design and belief of what is optimal for performance. Some manufacturers distribute the weight more in the head of the racket while others believe in a center weight for balance, and yet others believe in taking weight out of the head.

Game-improving rackets provide weaker players with more power. Thicker beams and improved materials such as titanium, ceramics, and basalt are just some of the components used in today's rackets that amp up the power potential. Oversized heads are also easier to hit with and provide bigger "sweet spots" for those players who don't hit it perfectly every time. Nothing like a little forgiveness in a racket.

Good players benefit from thinner beams and spin technology in the stringing patterns. The added power of a weaker player's racket is not always a good thing for the big hitters in today's power game. Smaller head sizes are faster through the air and can create their own power. Really good players have both power and variety in their games, and the racket is like a magic wand in their hand.

One of the most anticipated new racket releases is going on right now. Roger Federer has switched rackets, and the wait for his new frame, the Wilson Pro Staff RF97 Autograph, is over. After going through 127 prototypes, Federer is switching to a more modern racket in hopes of gaining more power to keep up with younger, stronger hitters. His racket is not for everyone, though. Most of you would think it is too heavy with too small of a head. He seems to have no trouble hitting the center of the racket, and the additional weight, once he gets it moving, adds the power needed at his level.

The bottom line is you need to demo a new racket soon. Otherwise your friend with his or her new frame may bury you. Come try the new Pro Staff Federer racket at Seaside Tennis and see if it is the correct one for your game.

'Tis the Season to Adjust Your Tennis Game

originally published November/December 2014

It's fall, and the weather in Seaside is great for tennis. Winter is just around the corner. The temperature has dropped, and the breeze is blowing. Even the sun doesn't have that same intensity. And the days are shorter, too. All of this will affect your tennis game.

Remember that the cooler temps require a longer warm-up. It takes most of us a little longer to get going when the mercury drops. Be sure to go through the tennis swing completely to stretch everything out to prevent injury. Strings will break more often, and really cold weather will change the bounce of the ball.

The wind blowing the leaves around also blows the tennis ball around. Wind is one of the biggest influences on the flight of a tennis ball. Embrace it and learn to use it to your advantage. It helps the speed of the ball when it's behind you. It helps the spin of the ball when you are hitting into it. And it will keep the ball in or blow the ball out when it gusts or swirls across the court. You should always know which way the wind is blowing to make needed adjustments.

In addition to the reduced intensity, the sun also hangs lower in the sky this time of year. It seems to be right in your line of sight more since it is not high in on the horizon like it is in the summer. The sun is also a huge influence on you and your opponent. Changeovers keep the sun from being unfair to one player or the other, but the player who handles the sunny side best seems to fare better at the end. Adjustments will have to be made to your toss, and sometimes your stance, to prevent the blinding effect the sun can have.

Shorter days mean night play is needed from time to time, too. Lights make the ball look different and also cause sight issues when playing at night. Even the night air seems to affect all aspects of your tennis game. It feels moist, and the balls seem to get heavier.

We are fortunate to live in such a great climate for fall and winter tennis. Look at the weather in other areas of the country and be thankful you have the opportunity to play all winter outside. And most days here in Seaside are sunny. Oh, yeah, that can be a problem. What a great problem you have here for your tennis game!

Use the Yellow Ball to Win Your Tennis Match

originally published January/February 2015

As I write this column, it is about 72 and sunny here in Seaside, in December. It is the reason we have all come here. How could anyone not love the weather this beautiful day?

But on the tennis court, this sunny day can present a problem for your opponents if you know how to use it. The sun will hang lower in the sky from about November to March here at the beach. If you have the sun in your eyes, it can really be blinding.

The first way to use the sun is to lob more. Most players don't turn enough to get the sun out their eyes. Most players don't use their nondominant hand to shield the sun from their view. Most players just hit a weak overhead when the sun is in their eyes.

Second, simply loft more shots. Don't hit a high lob but try instead to add a few feet of net clearance with a little less pace on some of your ground strokes and let the ball bounce up toward the sun. You will be amazed at the number of mishits this will cause.

Third, look for the lefty. If a team has a left-handed player on the sunny side, hit it to them every shot (unless it's Rafa). They have a sun-blinded view of nearly every forehand they hit, and it will frustrate them to no end. And since most players have a bigger forehand than backhand, it will take away that advantage.

Fourth, plan on hitting a bigger return. Players tossing the serve up into the sun will rarely hit a good serve consistently. Take full advantage of this. After all, this is the one time that you know where the ball is going to be hit. It is going to be hit in that square right in front of you and probably not hit as effectively as usual because of that "big yellow ball" shining right in their eyes.

It is great to have a third player on your side in doubles, and if you use the sun correctly, it will feel like you have just that. I've never met anyone that the sun did not bother in some way. Remember though that this advantage only lasts for two games at a time, and then you'll have to switch sides with your opponents. Hopefully they did not read this article.

What's Your Style

originally published March/April 2015

I want to talk to you about style. And I don't mean clothes. Do you know what style of tennis you play? My Wilson rep recently showed me their new racket technology customized for the three styles of play: the baseliner, the attacker, and the net player.

Baseliners are people who never come to the net unless they have to. They are fast on their feet and hover just behind the baseline for every shot. They are consistent, patient, and in good shape. They don't take a lot of chances. They wait for their opponents to make the mistakes, and they make few mistakes themselves. Baseliners hit the ball deep in the court, and they have the ability to stay on the court as long as it takes to wear you out.

Attackers look to take advantage of short balls or mistakes. They drive the ball into a corner and follow it in. They take more risks on short balls and hit more aggressively more often. Balls that float toward them will be taken out of the air with an offensive volley that they follow in to the net. The attacker likes overheads and typically puts them away.

Net players live at the net. They have good volleys and good overheads. They are quick, and they plan ways to get to the net whenever they are at the baseline. They can chip and charge, or they can slice the ball and move forward. A net player is always looking for a way to take the ball out of the air. They serve and volley, always follow a lob to the net, and have effective approach shots.

Most of the pros you see on tour stay back on the baseline.

Very few true serve-and-volley players are left. Even the attackers have to be picky about what shots they come in behind.

You have to recognize what style tennis you play in order to improve. I love to beat players by making them do something they are uncomfortable doing or are unable to do. If you don't know what kind of player you are, come see me. And if you do know what kind of player you are, come see me. We have some work to do either way.

Put a Little Seaside in Your Tennis Game

originally published May/June 2015

Seaside has a beat that is slower than most places. Folks are relaxed, and time seems to slow down. This laid-back atmosphere is a change of pace for most visitors. Changing up your pace is also a great way to make your tennis game better.

Everyone moves at his or her own pace. On the tennis court, it is easy to see who is high strung and who is not; who likes to hit it hard and who likes to hit it slowly; and who likes to play fast and who takes their time. Change of pace seems to disrupt almost everyone.

If I am playing really well and yet I am still losing, I try to play "not so well." This means instead of hitting a really good ball that my opponent is not having any trouble with, I add spin, add pace, or take pace off the ball. Try looping a slow ball deep into the court and see if you can disrupt the timing of the player on the other side of the net. Spin a ball to them and see how they react. Hit one really hard right up the middle of the court, over the low part of the net, and see if they have the time to produce a shot with your ball's added speed.

Spin is produced by friction between the ball and the strings. Hitting with spin changes the speed of the ball. Balls hit with topspin kick forward on the bounce, which gives an opponent less time to swing through the ball. It can bounce higher into an opponent's weaker hitting zones. And it promotes the ball dipping down into the court at the last second on shots landing near the lines. Backspin or slice has the opposite bounce, seeming to almost stop or even back up when it hits the court. Backspin balls can skid or stay low when hit hard enough, which creates real issues for opponents who have trouble getting under the ball.

Speed needs no explanation. Increased speed cuts down on your opponent's ability to get to the ball. It may also require them to shorten their own stroke or just block the ball back. Decreasing speed is often underrated. Big hitters like pace coming at them to generate even bigger shots with more power. Slowing a ball down will often drive these players crazy. They overhit shots. They have more mishits. They are way out in front of the ball and they pull it out of bounds. And the one I like the most, it frustrates them. They think the weak shot should be killed, and most players cannot do it consistently enough to win.

The next time you are back home on the court and losing, I want you to think of Seaside. Slow down. Try something new. Relax. And "change the pace."

3 Tennis Myths Explained

originally published July/August 2015

Every pro you've ever taken a lesson from was truly trying to help you understand the game of tennis better. Tennis professionals often repeat sayings they think will stick with you. Some things get lost in the translation from their mouths to your brain, though. Let's look at three tennis myths most players have engrained in their brains.

You've all heard "watch the ball," right? Well, that's not exactly true. What you need to watch is your opponent hitting the ball. You need to see what spin is coming at you. You need to see how much net clearance the ball has to figure out where to move to hit the ball. You do need to watch the ball to make good contact, but you probably won't actually see it. The ball is traveling too fast and the swing is too quick to see actual contact.

My favorite myth is "stay out of no man's land." First of all, to get from the baseline to the net position, you have to go through this zone. You usually have to hit a ball from there as you move to the net. I believe you should spend vast amounts of time in practice learning to manufacture shots better from this area. Work on picking up difficult half-volleys. Work on taking a volley out of the air and moving up into the court. Work on your overhead from this area since it's where overheads are hit. This mid-court area is the best zone for you to be in as far as court coverage goes. Your opponent can't lob it over your head if you are standing between the service line and the baseline, and you can cover most balls landing in front of you. Most everyone I know tends to move forward better than they do backward. I'm not telling you to live in no man's land, but work hard on improving your game there.

"Forehand has the middle," right? What if your partner has a better backhand than your forehand? What if your partner is left-handed and you are right-handed and you both have forehands? My advice is to get over the forehand thing; whoever can get to the ball first and get it back to the other side first should take it. Cut down your opponent's recovery time by getting the ball back quickly. Tennis is about time. If you can improve the amount of time you have to prepare and hit the ball and cut down the time your opponent has to do the same thing, I'll bet you have more success.

These are just a few of the tennis myths that are commonly thought to be true. Come see me at the courts and we will talk about what sayings you've heard in your tennis career. We'll separate myth from fact. Bottom line, don't believe everything you hear from any pro without a good explanation.

Why Is There "Green Sand" on the Tennis Courts?

originally published September/October 2015

I have been around tennis almost all my life, so I forget that everyone has not experienced different court surfaces. I love it when hard court players come by Seaside Tennis and wonder what the green sand on the court is.

Our courts are made of Har-Tru, a manmade clay of sorts. It's actually crushed granite that is treated with a bonding agent so that it sticks together when damp. There are many benefits to this surface, especially in our climate. Our courts are Hydro-Courts, equipped with an underground watering system that runs constantly and allows us to have continuous play. The old aboveground systems sprayed water across the court surface where the wind could blow it away or cause flooding, which then required hours for drying before play could be resumed. Now we sweep the courts early in the morning, and play continues uninterrupted throughout the day.

Clay courts are about 10 to 15 degrees cooler than a hard court in the heat. They are also easier on the body overall. Footing is a bit different as you usually slide a little as you step into each shot. This helps the body because you don't slam your foot into the hard court each time you take a step or hit a ball. The bounce on clay is also a little slower than that of a hard court, so it is easier to have a long rally. You do need experience playing on clay to feel comfortable with your footing and to understand how to construct the longer points.

Clients often ask me about the "grass court" in the picture

of former No. 1 Jim Courier and myself with the big Seaside windscreen in the background. In 2005, we turned the croquet lawn into a grandstand grass court! The court had to be rolled and packed down over and over to ensure a relatively true bounce. You see this surface at the prestigious Wimbledon tournament every summer. These courts have to be watered, mowed, and rolled similar to a putting green. You don't see many grass courts anymore simply because they are so hard to maintain. Play on grass courts requires great quickness as the ball doesn't bounce as high and tends to skid more. Volleys are more prevalent, and pushing off on the grass is tricky as well. But, it is a great surface to experience if you can find a grass court for a match.

Hard courts are and will remain the most used court surface. They are easier to build, cheaper to maintain and more durable. The upcoming US Open is played on a hard court as are most of the tennis tournaments in the amateur circuits. Even this surface has some variety, with some surfaces softer than others depending on the mix of the court material. The bounce is true and the footing is more secure, although it pounds the body more than other surfaces.

Have a good time playing on the various surfaces, and come play with me in the "green sand" sometime.

Tennis Time!

originally published November/December 2015

Tennis is a great game, and this time of year is my favorite for playing. The weather has finally cooled off, and the courts are more pleasant all day long for matches. Whatever time of year you play, what is your "time" on the court like?

Time on the court varies for different players. You can get in a quick workout with a hitting partner, on the ball machine, or in a private lesson. Or, if you have the time, you can play several sets with your playing partners. You can speed up play by hitting harder and being more aggressive to end points quickly. Conversely, you can stay on the baseline, have long rallies, and extend play. Both styles are fun and effective, and you should try both to see which fits you and your personality.

Your personality has more to do with your time on the court than you might think. If you are really uptight on the court, it can affect your play. Remember watching McEnroe on the courts years ago? He seemed to be mad almost all the time, but he still played great. On the other hand, Borg was as calm as could be, and his icy emotions seemed to impact his opponents way more than him. The reason Borg and McEnroe played at such a high level was because of the time they had put in on and off the courts. Their training included short, intense workouts on the courts, and at other times, they ran long miles to increase their endurance.

Time of day is a factor in your tennis game, too. Do you play after work or in the mornings before work? Or do you only get to play on weekends? Or only when you vacation in Seaside? I know all of these player types, and the time of day they play enters into their playing style. People that have worked all day are there to blow off steam and relax. The morning players always seem like they have somewhere they're supposed to be. The weekend warriors and the vacationers actually look like they are having the most fun.

Your tennis is affected by time. Make the most of it on the court, and, above all, savor that time. It truly is a fun game if you will take the "time" to enjoy it!

Can a Beach Day Improve Your Tennis Game?

originally published January/February 2016

You are here at Seaside on vacation, and you can only spend so much time on the tennis courts before your family gets mad. And you wouldn't want to miss a beach day with your family anyway. How can you improve your tennis game from our beautiful beaches? I know a few ways.

First, you have all seen the paddle tennis that kids play on the beach. Pick up one of these fun sets at the toy store, and you'll be the family hero for playing with your spouse and the kids while you improve your volleys. Hand and eye coordination will improve from just keeping the ball off the sand. Don't forget to use the correct technique and footwork, and have some fun by trying to keep a rally going for 10 to 20 hits. Do it over and over with different opponents (I mean different kids). It's good to see a different volley come back at you, making you adjust to keep a rally going.

Second, throw the football with the kids or your buddy on the beach. It is almost the same as a service motion. The wrist snap needed to make the ball spiral is close to the same motion you use to hit a serve. Try to throw right over the top of your shoulder like you would on a serve. Transfer your weight forward in the sand as you release the ball. Reach back and "throw it long" once in a while to increase your flexibility and increase pace on a serve. Be accurate and throw the ball at your target like you would serve at a target.

Third, throw the Frisbee. It is close to a backhand motion.

Let the wrist snap as you release and notice how it feels similar to a topspin backhand. Though not exactly the same, the motion will help stretch you out, and the release may even help you to follow through better on the court.

And lastly, just run around and have fun with the kids. Your endurance will improve as you get in multiple beach days. Run sprints by playing chase and improve your cutting skills and footwork. Your balance should improve after you fall in the shifting sands a few times as well.

"Yours!" Really?

originally published March/April 2016

I love it when my partner says "yours" right after it goes by and I have no chance to react. Has that ever happened to you? What I should ask is, how many times does that happen to you in a game?

I encourage players to play doubles like they do singles. Get everything you can and really over-cover the middle of the court. Be active and aggressive when you can and help your partner, not just take up space and rely on your partner.

Let's talk about the middle of the court. It is the safest area for your opponents to hit in because it is over the lowest part of the net and it is the farthest distance from out of bounds. It confuses the enemy on the other side, and it requires one of the players to take the shot in the middle. "Yours!"

I think both players should over-cover the middle. Make the opponents hit the alleys where it's nearer out of bounds over the higher part of the net. I'll bet you draw more errors this way. Also, don't be afraid to cut in front of your partner and hit a winner. Be aggressive and have some fun. It cuts down on your opponent's reaction time, too, if you can get the ball back to their side quicker.

I think both players on a team should "hug" the middle of the court. Give the appearance that the middle is covered and make the opponents go somewhere else. And be mentally leaning toward that "somewhere else" to cover that part of the court as well. It will drive the opponents crazy.

And get out and play singles once a week for practice. It improves your rhythm, it makes you cover every ball, it gets you in better shape, and maybe most importantly, there is no one to yell "yours!" at.

Hope to see you on the courts soon. Come by the pro shop for any of your tennis needs. Or set up a lesson with one of our great pros. We will help you to cure all bad habits.

Tennis Fashion

originally published May/June 2016

Those of you who know me are laughing right now after reading that I am writing about tennis fashion. Thanks to my wife dressing me, I actually have on matching shorts and shirts most of the time. This edition, I want to talk about how the new fashion is helpful to your performance.

Remember playing in cotton tee shirts and shorts or skirts and tops that were made of thick, heavy polyester? I think those cotton tees weighed about five pounds when wet. Today's clothing is moisture wicking and dries almost as quickly as it gets wet. Players stay cooler on the court, and the fabrics allow your body to better recover even while wearing wet clothing. Several manufacturers are making apparel with UV protection built in to help protect you from the harsh sun. And they weigh nothing. Shorts are made with built-in underwear and skirts with built-in tights for more warmth when needed.

Fashion today looks good, too. I remember wearing a pair of the lined denim shorts that Andre Agassi played in. They looked good, but they were extremely hot and very heavy when wet. Players like to feel good about the way they look, which can really affect how they play. Today's clothing companies have combined aesthetics with functionality, and we are all benefitting from their ingenuity.

Footwear has also come a long way. Today's shoes have more support and yet are more comfortable than the shoes of the past. And they, too, are more fashionable and colorful than ever before. Some companies even allow you to personalize and customize your shoes.

And accessories have gotten in on the act. Performance material caps and UV protecting hats now exist. Socks and sweatbands come in colors and patterns yet have improved performance as well. Warm-ups have zip out sleeves that will turn into a vest and pants that convert into shorts so you can adjust to your own body temperature.

Look in your closet at your current tennis wardrobe and decide if you are in need of an upgrade. It can really help your game. And then come see me, or I should say my wife who runs our tennis shops, for some good advice.

What's Your Position

originally published July/August 2016

I love it when I am asked the best place to stand on the tennis court. My answer is pretty much always the same. I think the overall best place to be positioned on the court is one step inside the service line.

Let's talk about the four positions that exist. Most people love the baseline position. The power of today's game requires most people to stand just behind the baseline and bang ground strokes until someone makes a mistake. I can't argue that this is the way the game has been moving for some time. Even in doubles, I sometimes coach both players on a doubles team to start at the baseline and work their way into the net position. Playing singles almost always makes you stay back on the baseline because of the power of today's rackets, which provide maximum depth and pace on ground strokes.

The next area forward of the baseline is the infamous no man's land. I know you have heard to avoid this area like the plague because of the awkward shots you have to hit from this area. And while it is true that no man's land is awkward, I actually think it should be practiced more than any other area! You are absolutely going to get caught here and should be prepared to manufacture shots to the best of your ability. The only way to get comfortable from this position is with a lot of practice and reps. In many of our drills we have you transition through this treacherous area in an attempt to make you more comfortable and confident in no man's land. Not only that, but as far as court coverage goes, no man's land might be the best overall position for covering the most court.

The next area is my favorite, just inside the service line. You can step in and be aggressive on a volley. You can cover nearly all lobs, and you're not so close that a lob goes over you or that you get blasted. You have enough time to easily get to any sort of drop shot. In addition, positioning yourself just inside the service line can be intimidating to your opponents.

The last position is the net position, which is about one to three feet away from the net. Many of you love this position, but you're too close. You had better put the first ball you hit away, or you are dead. Your opponent will go over you, around you or through you, and there is not much you can do about it unless you move like a superhero.

Try all positions on the court and see where you excel. You'll know quickly where you play well from and where you need work. Or come see me for a lesson, and I'll help you decide.

Friends for a Week

originally published September/October 2016

I arrived in Seaside in 2000 to become the director of tennis. I came from a membership-based club in Huntsville, Alabama, where I managed and taught for 13 years prior to coming to the 30A area. The differences in resort tennis and club tennis were evident right from the start. In club tennis, we teach the same people day in and day out, sometimes for years. I built great relationships with my clients who became my friends. We had the luxury of working on their tennis goals over time, and I loved seeing my players' games progress.

In my new resort setting, I learned quickly that I would have "friends for the week." People arrived, scheduled lessons, and played in clinics throughout the week. And then they were gone, and a new group arrived. This was my new tennis life, and I loved it.

Resort tennis is about having fun! Players are on vacation and are in a good mood. They are happy to get on the courts and are willing to try new things and play with new people. I immediately recognized that I would have to blend together players of all levels to have a successful resort program. I designed my clinics to keep people moving and to get them a good workout. For clinics, I have my pros feed live ball drills where players play out points. We take two or three quick water breaks, making sure all players hit a lot of balls and keep moving.

In our resort tennis program, we do the same drills almost every day. Returning players love that they know what is going on, and they help me explain the drills to the new players.

It makes people interact. And playing with the good players helps the not-so-good players improve. Players meet others with similar skill levels, and they set up their own matches through that interaction. The drills are varied enough that everyone finds a drill they like or a skill they need to work on. And in all of my years of doing the same drills, nobody has mastered them all yet.

All my 30A Tennis pros are excellent teaching professionals. They may teach different things and in different ways than I do, and that variety benefits our players. When a skill is taught or explained differently, players may finally "get it" in a way they haven't before. And where better to try something new than on vacation? Players can try new things in a fun setting with people they don't know and may never see again, so there's nothing to lose by giving it a try.

Besides teaching new things to new people, the key to my resort tennis program is making good players play with "not so good" players, and vice versa! It is great to play up with players better than yourself, and it is equally great to play with players that are where you were once. I love the interaction. And I can tell you, based on the size of my clinics and round robins and the smiles I see as you leave, that you get it, too! And now, I have "friends for a week" that return all the time.

New Year, New Game

originally published January/February 2017

The beginning of a new tennis season is always so exciting. It is a great opportunity to try out all the new things you've worked on in a real tennis match. Wait, you didn't improve anything during the off-season? All you did was play matches? No new weapons or at least fixes in your game?

Practice may be boring to some of you, but it is vital to improve your level of play. I also think it is important to try new things from time to time. Players that don't improve over time seem to lose ground. You have all heard you are either improving or getting worse, and I think that is true.

New aspects of your game should be introduced slowly and always with a pro or at least a helpful eye. I want you to understand right up front that you mortals should not always be trying the things you see on television. And I caution all you pros who are not as smart as I am, be careful what you teach and to whom. We are trying to grow the game, which means we need to keep people playing and healthy. Some clients and students simply cannot do some things, and we professionals should help them to understand that. Choose your pro wisely!

By no means do I ever want to limit a player's progress. But I want people to understand that progress is usually slow and takes work. Sometimes a player is limited by an old injury, conditioning, a lack of strength in certain areas, or any number of things. A simple grip change may require a different swing, using different muscles, and a different follow-through. Many "improvements" are for special situations and require many hours of instruction and repetition to master a shot that you can add to your arsenal. Additions are just that. Remember when working on a new shot not to lose a current shot. I never try to completely change someone's game.

New grips, better conditioning, different or improved follow-through, new shot patterns, improved touch shots, new serves or different serves, and new tactics are just a few ways to improve your game. Trying to work on all of these might overload the computer and the body. Pick one or two things to work on at a time and stick with them. Change or improvement can take many practice sessions to show progress. I think you have to "make" a new shot at least 10 times to "own it." And I think it probably takes a hundred "misses" to make those 10. Stay on course and don't get discouraged.

Finally, as always, I encourage having fun with your new toys. New shots will be missed from time to time. I don't miss them, but you probably will! Take that fun attitude with you and just keep swinging. The reward is coming if you put in the work. I promise.

Coming Home

originally published March/April 2017

In 2000, I was hired by Seaside as the new tennis director. I remember driving down 30A from Grayton Beach and coming upon this beautiful oasis of a town. The town was much quieter then, and the program was slow. I built a thriving resort tennis program for the community and called this place home. Then I moved out of state for a few years for family reasons, later returning to the area, but to another resort.

I am proud to announce that I am coming home, back to Seaside. While my company, 30A Tennis, continues to manage other resort facilities, I will be offering my tennis programming exclusively in Seaside.

Seaside has always been the leader on 30A, hosting many of the area's activities, concerts, plays, parades, and art events. This is the place where I want to teach. I'll be devoting all my time and efforts to current and new programming, available only in Seaside.

We have morning adult clinics and round robins throughout the year. Spring and summer are crazy busy, and additional clinics are added for those peak times to meet the needs of the town. After-school programs run fall, winter, and spring. Off-season events include ladies' team weekends and mixers, and summer programs will be available for everyone's June to August travel schedules.

Some of you may remember when we staged a Wimbledon-style event featuring former world No. 1 player Jim Courier. Seaside's croquet lawn was transformed into a grass court, where spectators packed the grandstands for exhibition play. I got to play Courier in a lopsided match (guess who won?) and conduct a clinic with him on the grass for our guests. Look for more of these types of events to return.

Our tennis pro shop is second to none, and is the only store that offers Seaside Tennis logo merchandise. The latest fashions from the top tennis brands can be found in our shop along with rackets and stringing services. All my pros are excellent players and coaches and are trained to help you in all aspects of improving your game.

I truly believe Seaside founders Robert and Daryl Davis have created a very special place here, and I am honored that my tennis program will be a part of this community and all that is uniquely Seaside. I enjoy talking to you at Bud & Alley's Waterfront Restaurant about your lame forehand over a Red Stripe, or being stopped on my weekend beach walk to demonstrate a topspin backhand with no racket and a volleyball, or being attacked at dinner at Great Southern Café by the fun group of kids I taught earlier in the day. Where else in the world does this incredible atmosphere exist?

The other resorts are nice, but they are not and never will be Seaside. I'm happy to be back on Seaside's courts and look forward to seeing you there.

Get a Grip on Your Game

originally published May/June 2017

How one thing can improve your tennis game now! One change can improve you game? Really? Yes, really. So how about making five changes? Can you get five times better? Maybe! How you hold the racket is one of the most basic and important aspects of your game. The problem is there is no one correct grip that creates every shot.

Beginners usually pick up the racket, swing it, and get stuck with the grip they chose that first time. Depending on the success they have with that initial swing, their game forms and develops. That swing is one of your most important. Swings are hard to change, and every different swing should probably have a different grip for success.

Let's talk about the basic grips. The continental grip is about as basic as it gets. Today's modern game rarely ever uses this grip except for a serve and maybe an overhead or volley. Swinging volleys have changed that, too.

Other variations are eastern, western, semi-western, and grips that don't really even have a name. Grips are produced by shot selection, court position, choice of pace or power, choice of spin, and any number of variables. If you ask me to show you my forehand grip, I have to ask you what spin you want me to hit at what pace from what court position. Complicated, right?!

That is why I think you may get five times better if you are willing to work hard and adapt to grip changes. Players unwilling to change grips for various shots are limiting their ability to improve. Look on tour at the extreme grips players have to use to produce certain shots. Now is a great time to watch all the different players and the shots they produce. Really notice their preparation and the grip changes they make.

Here is what I think you should do, and this is what I have my students do when they come for a lesson. "Tweak" your grip a little bit. Either way. And watch the outcome. Figure out how to the get the ball in the court in various ways with various spins. Do it consistently and watch how much you improve. It's easier said than done, though. Grip changes are difficult and take a lot of practice and time to change and master.

Making five changes at once would most likely destroy your game, so I would never do that to anyone at one time. But if you are serious about getting better, come see me or one of my pros and let us help you make ONE good change. And then maybe another one another time. And somewhere down the line you may just be five times better than you are right now!

Serve It Up

originally published July/August 2017

love watching the best players in the world serve when they are in trouble in a tournament. How many times have you seen Roger Federer down love–40, and then he pulls out three aces to bring it back to deuce? The top players, at least the top 25, all seem to have the ability to serve themselves out of trouble.

I hate watching some of the lower ranked players double fault at key moments to lose a game or even a set or match. It is truly painful to watch a double fault knowing the work these players have put in. I find it amazing that they've reached the career level they have with a weakness that can be so costly. They are young and working on improving, and so should you. Sometimes the part that is missing in the serve is simply between the ears.

I have some helpful advice for those of you who suffer the same serving pain in your matches: Repetition. I see some really crazy service motions at the tennis courts, but what I have noticed is that, like on TV, some of these motions hold up under pressure, and some don't. The consistent servers have an advantage, simply because they never donate a point. A double fault is like starting down love–15. So many matches hinge on just a point or two, so giving up a point is just painful.

Back to the advice: Get on the court with a basket of balls and work on your serve! I highly recommend a lesson first to improve your technique. All servers are different. There is no ONE correct way. Watch the pros with good serves. Their motions are not all the same, and yet they are all effective.

Watch the bad servers, too. They don't look fluid. They have "hitches" in their motion, and they lack confidence.

Repetition builds confidence. It makes your motion more fluid, and in a match, you have to be able to repeat that same motion over and over while under pressure. Why is your second serve so much weaker than your first serve? I say it is lack of confidence. How do you solve that? Repetition. Repetition. Repetition.

There are entire books written on the serve, and I can't go into all the facets of serving in this short article. But having a bad serve is unacceptable to me. Go see a pro. Work on your toss (I know it's bad!). Work on your stance; it can be improved. Keep your arm moving. Why have a "hitch" that is ugly and feels bad? There are so many things you can do to improve your serve, but the biggest thing that helps is REPETITION. See you on the courts!

Love Hurts

originally published September/October 2017

Tennis is a great game. We all know and agree on that. But the game we love can also cause us to experience some pain or soreness from time to time. Most days, I have someone complain of a pain or discomfort with some body part. I am no doctor, but I can sometimes help.

Frequently, pain comes from the elbow. Carpenters are the most common sufferers of tennis elbow, typically brought on by the overuse of a hammer or screwdriver. Those same motions are used over and over by tennis players as well. The spins we create using the elbow and wrist are simply hard on an arm. Over time, our muscles develop and become stronger. We can still strain them occasionally, and this can cause aggravating arm pain.

Some things can be done to help tennis elbow. Make sure you have the proper grip size on your racket. You may need to go up or down in size to best fit your hand. Try loosening your string tension next time you have your racket strung. You can even go to a softer string, which is what I recommend for most all my clients. And above all, check with a pro to make sure your motion is sound and you aren't going to further injure your arm with a bad swing. Rest is also sometimes mandatory for recovery, though I know most players do not want to hear that.

Knee pain is another common complaint. The pounding and change of direction required in a typical match is more wear and tear than the normal knee is used to. As you train and get in better shape, these pains go away or at least subside.

Strength training can help, too. Proper footwear is essential. Make sure you're wearing tennis shoes that provide support where it's needed. Shoes wear out, so replace yours when they lose their cushion. Playing on a softer surface like the clay courts we have in Seaside is easier on your knees and body as a whole.

And what about your back? Do you think it is normal for a body to turn violently from side to side over and over for a couple of hours? The torque you put on your body with a good tennis swing is rough on a back. Please be sure to stretch before and after each tennis session you have. Try strength training for this area, too. And work on your technique to ensure no further damage is done.

Other pains also arise, and most can be cured with proper training, rest, and some common sense. And schedule a lesson with one of our pros to assess your form and improve your comfort. Hope to see you on the courts soon, and please do tell us of your pains. Sometimes, we can actually help.

Lesson, Clinic, or Round Robin

originally published November/December 2017

Seaside Tennis has a variety of programs for club members and guests alike. We offer private instruction, group lessons, clinics, round robins, and team weekends, along with court rentals. What is the right choice for you?

A lesson gives you individual attention. You or your group can decide what you want to work on, and we can be specific with your drills. The pros will spend time on technique and strategy to develop a certain aspect of your game. Groups of people are more difficult because of the different skill sets players have. I view a lesson as a great opportunity to work on individual needs and wants. Beginners should do more lessons to get their games ready for play. Even the touring pros have coaches, and they all work on very specific skills in order to improve.

A clinic is a group of players that usually don't know each other. Typically, they don't have the same set of skills, and levels might be different. I design clinics to be fun and give you a good workout while working on a variety of skills. Some players are better at some shots than others, and that is the beauty of it: Players who are not as good at certain skills get to see how it should be done in play, and then they get chance after chance to work on improving that skill. Clinic instruction is general, and some strategy is involved. The key here is repetition. We do live ball drills where we start the point with a particular goal in mind. As that point develops, different things happen, just like in real tennis. Once a point begins, the ability to adapt becomes key.

Our round robin format is a little different in that we offer instructional round robins. You will play for time periods, usually five or six games with a partner. Then we bring you in, give instruction for the next round, and send you back out with a different partner against different opponents. We mix levels and genders. As you play, our pros walk around, watch points, and give instruction. Those of you who know me know that I "pick" on everyone equally, all in the name of fun.

Our custom team weekends are quite popular. And we have groups that return year after year. We customize these team trips for each group: Some groups want more beach time while others want a more tennis-intensive schedule. We only offer these in the off-season. And there's not much of an off-season anymore. Contact me if you want to get your group on the schedule for next year.

For those who want to play tennis with their friends and families, we offer court reservations for members and guests. We've got balls, rackets, shoes, and everything you need to play the game. Whatever your idea of tennis fun is, come see us at Seaside Tennis.

Aim "Out"

originally published January/February 2018

A tennis court is 78 feet long. It is 27 feet wide for singles and 36 feet wide for doubles. I'll bet some of you never knew the exact dimensions, and I am not sure that it really matters. Everyone can see the lines. (Except that last opponent you had!)

Let me tell you a "Tracyism" that has helped me my entire career: Sometimes, I aim out. Usually I do this in practice. But occasionally, I'll aim out in match if I am under pressure. I've learned that I can tighten up in big points. I've also learned that all points are big points. So aiming out sounds crazy, right?

In practice, since an out ball doesn't cost you an actual point, try aiming just beyond the lines. I'll bet that most of your "misses" actually land inside the lines, not out. The mind is a funny thing when it comes to playing tennis: Players tend to miss to the inside. Out is OUT, and we are trained to not hit the ball out.

I believe if you practice hitting shots more toward the outside, you can expand your hitting area. For doubles practice, imagine another alley outside the real alley and aim there. Watch where the ball lands. For singles practice, aim in the doubles alley and watch where it goes. I often do this with clients, and most of them err to the inside. In a playing situation, that means the ball is in the court, but you haven't stretched your opponent out to the full dimensions of the court.

It also helps to aim your serve out. Try this practice tip: Aim your first five serves at the baseline. Again, I'll bet you won't be able to hit it with your first five balls. What usually happens is your balls actually land in the service box or just beyond it. You're tight. Your mind sees the service box and wants to steer the ball there. If you hit your serve long with your first five practice serves, you accomplish two things. First, you stretch your shoulder out. And second, your mind sees the ball NOT hitting the net, which provides positive feedback.

If you are serving and down 30–40 in a match, aim a little long on your serve. Or if you're hitting a down-the-line passing shot, aim just beyond the line. Under pressure situations, these tactics have enabled me to hit a good, deep serve that actually lands in and to get the ball past the reach of my opponent instead of steering it too close to them.

You have to know your mind and how it works on the tennis court. I think I have already figured it out!

Let's Talk About MO!

originally published March/April 2018

T he next time you hit a winner, think about how you feel right in that moment. That's where momentum lives."

You all probably know that I consider my friend MO at Bud & Alley's the GOAT bartender, the Greatest of All Time. But that is not the MO I am talking about right now. While watching the Australian Open recently, the GOAT in tennis, Roger Federer in my opinion, grabbed MO in the fifth and final set to win his 20th major tennis championship. I am, of course, talking about MOmentum.

Tennis is an immensely taxing sport, both mentally and physically. I have played for over 40 years, and it always amazes me how momentum comes and goes in a match. In the match I was watching, Roger came out of the blocks fast and won the first set easily. He showed no signs of early nerves like his opponent did, and momentum was clearly on Roger's side.

The second set was really tight with both players settling into their comfort zones with only a few key points near the end of the set going the way of Marin Cilic, Roger's opponent. It really did seem that only a handful of points made the difference in the second set. So, you'd think Cilic has the momentum now, right?

The third set starts, and the shot-making and execution all swing back to Roger's favor. It's like he had forgotten or at least dismissed the last set and its unfavorable outcome in just a single changeover. Athletes have that ability to move past obstacles and focus on the task ahead, especially the great athletes.

Now the fourth set begins, and it seems that Roger might

have been looking ahead. He seems tentative at times, and his serve begins to really let him down. His serve, by the way, has always been one of his biggest and most dependable weapons. I have always admired how he can be down love–30 and then serve three aces to go up 40–30! Who does that? But not this set, and MO and the fourth set go to Cilic.

Now the fun begins. Both players only need to win one set to win the title. Both players can see the finish line. Both players now seem to have extra energy to get to the end. But again, MO switches back to Roger. He's very aggressive, playing to win and not even thinking about losing. His serve comes back to him. He starts hitting his targets again and getting free points that are demoralizing to an opponent. His opponent, on the other hand, seems to play not to lose, and MO from the fourth set leaves him almost immediately. The title goes to Federer!

The next time you hit a winner, think about how you feel right in that moment. I think that is where MO lives. Confidence is a fickle thing, but I believe that the confidence you get from practice and success is what enables you to create and maintain MOmentum. Come see me at the courts, and I'll share a few tips on creating and maintaining MO.

Teach Yourself!

Originally published May/June 2018

Here are some simple tips to help you help yourself. One of the best compliments I get is when a player tells me they "heard me in their head." I don't know that you want to hear my lovely singing voice in your head, but you do want to hear a voice of help and constructive criticism. Here are a few common scenarios and how you can teach yourself:

Tip #1: The ball goes long. The simple version is your racket is simply too open, or, better stated, is pointing toward the sky too much. Say to yourself, "You may need to add spin. You may need to lower the trajectory. Close the racket face slightly. You may need to take pace off. You may need to add more follow-through."

Tip #2: You are right-handed, and your forehand shot goes out to the right side of the court. Say to yourself, "You are late. The racket didn't get back out in front enough to steer the ball into the court. Shorten your backswing. Speed up your swing. Begin your swing earlier."

Tip #3: You are right-handed, and the forehand goes out to the left side of the court. Say to yourself, "You are early. The racket was too early, and contact pulled the ball out. Slow the swing down. Turn the body more in the beginning so you contact the ball slightly later. Try to start the swing later by letting the ball come a little past the early contact point."

Tip #4: The ball goes into the net. Say to yourself, "The racket face is probably too closed. You hit down on the ball too much. Try to stay down with your entire body as you hit the ball to promote an upward swing. Follow through in a higher position. Open up your racket face slightly."

Hitting the ball long, wide, and into the net are basic errors, and you can teach yourself how to fix them. Listen to that voice in your head telling what adjustments to make. It can be more complicated, but I always think you should look at the most simple fix first. Think of all the problems you are having on the court with any shot, and then backtrack to see if you can come up with a solution.

What I see time and time again is the same scenario playing out on the court and a player doing nothing to fix the problem. You should and must teach yourself how to handle various problems during a match. If you can't figure it out, come see me, and we will work it out together.

A New Era for Tennis?

originally published July/August 2018

An article in a recent issue of *Tennis* magazine featured a new format for tennis. Roger Federer and Lleyton Hewitt debuted this new format in Australia in 2015, and now the format is catching on worldwide, including here at Seaside This new format is called FAST4, and it is a quicker way to play tennis.

All sports struggle with the time commitment factor. Golf takes four or five hours to complete a round. They are now promoting Play 9 instead. Baseball is trying to keep batters in the box and limiting mound visits to shorten the length of the game. Football has put in special rules for overtime to try to end games earlier. Basketball instituted a shot clock to try to speed up play. And tennis is no different. Traditional scoring can have a single game going for an unlimited amount of time with deuce and ad possibilities. Remember Isner vs. Mahut at Wimbledon and their match that lasted over eleven hours?

FAST4 is a faster way to play tennis with four rules: There's no advantage scoring, the first to four games wins, a tiebreaker is played at three games all, and service lets are played. Even the tiebreaker is shortened: The first to five points wins. And you can even do a tiebreaker for the third set instead of another complete set to four. FAST4 lets you set your own rules ahead of time to work with time constraints. I can easily see this format or something similar being adopted for league tennis in the future.

I run an extremely busy tennis program at one of the best and busiest vacation destinations in the world. My thousands of tennis players want to play tennis, but they also want to go to the beach, ride bikes, shop, and have time to enjoy great restaurants with friends and family. The new FAST4 format lets me accommodate players' desires to do it all!

I started a FAST4 Ladies Day Out program at Seaside on a trial basis this spring, and it's met with great success already. Everyone seems to like the new, quick pace. And they like that they know that match play lasts for a predictable amount of time. Then we all head to Bud & Alley's for lunch! The learning curve for us old traditional players is easy and fun. I may even expand this program throughout the year.

Don't worry, though. All of our others programs still exist. I would never change a popular and successful program. But I love adding to it!

Hope to see you on the courts soon. I mean "FAST!"

Tennis Season in Seaside

originally published September/October 2018

We often get asked what's going on at Seaside Tennis. The answer depends on what time of year you're inquiring about. Although we do not get fall foliage or spring cherry blossoms in Seaside, we do have our seasons.

When I arrived in 2000, I immediately saw the need to establish programs for the tennis part of visits to Seaside. For 18 years, I've been helping families and groups have a perfect tennis experience on their vacations. Different groups want and need different tennis programs, and the way we cater to those needs changes throughout the year.

In the spring, days are shorter. And entire families are here together on spring break, sometimes with friends in tow. We run after-school programs for our local kids. And we plug resort guest juniors into open spots. Morning clinics and round robins are for the adults while the kids are still sleeping (it is spring break after all). Play for families is available throughout the day, whether it's taking a lesson or having a family match.

Summer brings longer days. But they are very warm. Early morning clinics for adults allow them to beat the daytime heat and get back to the family by mid-morning. Our junior program is also moved earlier in the day to late morning. Kids can sleep in but still get up and get in some tennis before the family lunch date. Advanced young players can set up private hitting times with me or one of my pros to keep up their skills while still on vacation. I do believe in giving these young players some time for things other than just tennis. Nothing is better than beach time with their friends. A bonus is that you can play much later with late summer sunsets. A friendly game of tennis after dinner is something to savor in the summer.

Fall has become a busy season with school fall breaks. Plus it's widely known as having the best weather of the year. It's also slow enough to allow us time to host weekend groups. We run our normal mornings for adults and afternoons for kids, but we can take groups or teams and conduct intense tennis getaways. We typically run these Friday through Sunday with added clinics, match play, and round robin play. We typically modify these packages to suit each group, from beach bonfires and catered lunches to massages and simply more court time.

Winter is just a word for us here in Seaside. It's not really a season. Our weather is good all year, so we still run daily programming, juniors, and weekend packages in the winter. It's actually the best time to do team weekends. The days are cool enough for really good workouts, and most leagues are between seasons. Skills can be added at this time when you are not so involved in league play. There's nothing like coming out in the spring with a new shot or weapon that old opponents have not seen.

Bottom line, I can help you plan your perfect tennis trip, no matter the season or your tennis goals. Are you a family? Are you a group? Do you want a lot of play or a little? Are you a beginner or an advanced player? Do you want private instruction or group instruction? And if you don't know a soul but want to play, I can take care of that, too. You just need to make a phone call or send me a text or email to get started on your perfect tennis trip.

Building Your Game from the Ground Stroke Up

originally published November/December 2018

The real basics of tennis begin with ground strokes. The ball bounces, and you hit it over the net. Then the ball bounces on the opposing side. Sounds simple, but it can be far more complicated than that. It all starts with your ground strokes.

A topspin ground stroke is the go-to choice for most all tennis players at all levels. Topspin ground strokes are done with a low to high swing. You can vary the height and depth of your shots, depending on the amount of spin you create with each stroke. The speed of the modern game favors the topspin ground stroke. The spin also adds safety to your shots because the ball tends to dip back down and bounce in the court on the opposing side instead of sailing out.

Backspin, or slice strokes, are also frequently used. The swing is the opposite of the topspin: A slice is a high to low swing. You can also vary this spin with the amount of loft you put on your racket at impact. A problem with the slice at high-speed play is the tendency for the ball to go up and too far out. It is much harder to control at accelerated speeds. A slice is a great way to diffuse power from the opposing side. You can cut off the power of a shot coming at you like a bullet by using backspin. A slice move allows a creative player to finesse "touch" on lobs and drop shots. A slice shot is also a little easier on the shoulder overall.

A flat stoke is seldomly used these days. It requires perfect timing and a low trajectory over the net. At the speed of today's game, it's hard to hit consistently. A flat stroke is basically straight back and straight through the ball. Good luck on this one. You may want to leave the flat stroke to the old-timers.

The bottom line is to get out on the courts and spend time developing your ground strokes. A variety of strokes provides the best arsenal on the court, but you may find that you're a specialist in one or the other of these styles of play.

Do you consistently hit with a topspin? Are you a slicer and dicer? Are you able to put together a variety of ground strokes to take your game to the next level? Come see me on the courts and let's see what type player you are.

And I almost forgot to mention one of the great benefits of knocking around ground strokes over and over: It is a great stress reliever!

Court Care for Everyone

originally published January/February 2019

I get compliments on our courts here at Seaside often. I think without great courts you cannot have a great program. I put a lot of time and effort into keeping my courts in the best shape possible. Everyone that walks on the tennis court though can help keep courts in shape. I see my clients helping all the time.

The best way to pack a court down is to have tons of play. A thousand footsteps in tennis shoes act as a means of packing and leveling the court. We are lucky here at Seaside to have a robust program year-round so we do get that aid from our players in maintaining the courts. We also have a professional crew come in once a quarter to make sure enough material is down and to further pack the courts down once this new material is added.

The edge of that same tennis shoe that packs the court can also damage it though. Dragging a heal or the side of your shoe on the court can be fixed almost immediately however with the bottom of your shoe. Just rake across the bad indention with the bottom of your shoe and you can smooth out the court surface. This also helps you to not get a bad bounce should a ball hit the same spot. It is like fixing a ball mark on a putting green where the golf ball has landed and has left an indention.

Fixing these marks immediately is not only good for the court or the green but is a courtesy to all.

The shoe itself can be good or bad for the court. Flat-soled shoes are required for play on clay courts. Shoes that are not flat can tear up and scar the courts and are also dangerous for your ankles. A ribbed bottom could catch on a line and stop sliding as it should and injure an ankle. Track or running shoes have very uneven bottoms and are also sometimes elevated. These are probably the worst on the courts and your ankles on a tennis court. Shoes are made for specific sports, and you should really make sure for safety's sake that you have on the right shoe for the right sport.

I've only talked about our soft court here at Seaside, but hard courts need proper care as well. Debris and leaves can become very hazardous if left on any court. Wet courts are especially dangerous whether hard or soft. Lines on both hard and soft courts are seemingly always more slippery. Summer heat can turn a hard court into a stove top feel to any bare skin that hits it and should always be avoided.

The bottom line I think for all players though is to maintain or at least help maintain any court you play on. Know the risks of any court surface and prepare accordingly. Think of the players coming on the court behind you and try to help them with their playing experience. Hope the players in front of you did the same. Playing or teaching though, I still smooth out blemishes in the court. Pick up and remove a pebble or a stick. Walk the leaf off the court. If every player does this you will always have a better court to play on.

Spring Forward

originally published March/April 2019

In the spring, time moves forward. As tennis players, we would all benefit by springing forward, too.

Spring correlates with tennis in several ways. The color of spring is green, and so are most courts. Spring is when flowers emerge and new leaves sprout. It's also the time you should be blooming on the tennis court since all league and school schedules are in full force.

Spring is a happy season, and I guarantee you'll have more success on the court if you keep a positive, happy attitude. Spring is a vibrant, growing season. Think of your game the same way.

How can springing forward help your tennis game? Springing into the ball provides more pace. On ground strokes, step into the ball and lean your body forward out over the ball. You'll see that you can hit it harder. I tell people daily you're bigger than the ball, don't let it push you back.

After you hit the ball, spring forward to put pressure on your opponent. This puts you into an offensive position. Spring up after every shot as you make your split-step. Then you're prepared to spring forward on the next shot. Spring forward into your volleys for put-away winners.

A spring in my step gives me an advantage, both physically and mentally. Opponents hate to look across the net and see energy from you. It seems to zap some of their energy. A good spring mentally and physically puts you on offense and in control.

Seaside Tennis's schedule bursts with activity in the spring.

School tennis teams, spring breakers, league players, and migrating snowbirds are all on the courts looking for an edge. I like to tell all my players that putting spring into their game is a way to get ahead.

Come see me or one of my pros for a lesson on springing forward. Happy spring!

Hit the Wall

originally published May/June 2019

Can hitting the wall improve your tennis game? I'm not talking about when you're having a physical or mental block. I mean actually hitting the ball against the tennis hitting wall at Seaside!

Seaside is one of the few tennis facilities that has a hitting wall. Some call it a backboard and think of it as old-school. Fancy ball machines are the newer thing, and we have that at Seaside, too. But I grew up hitting against a wall, and it can benefit you, too.

There is a big green fiberglass backboard right in front of you. There is a line drawn on the wall representing the height and slope of the net. You can stand as close or as far away as you see fit. It actually requires a good bit of control and strategy.

The harder you hit the ball into wall, the harder it comes back. The higher you hit on the wall, the higher it comes back. The more cross-court you hit on the wall, the more cross-court the ball is returned. Control is a must in order to keep the ball going. Control. What a great concept, right?!

The drills I use on the wall are simple but effective. First, stand about four feet from the wall to do volleys. Hit it straight ahead and soft enough in the beginning to do only forehands. Then only backhands. Then alternate. Then back up a few steps and speed things up.

These drills will only last a few seconds to begin with. It will wear you out! And you will see how little control you have at first. Like most things, practice makes it better.

Second, back up about twenty feet from the wall. Try to hit it straight enough to hit only forehands into the wall, but hit it soft enough to let it bounce twice before striking it again. This will require tons of footwork, tons of aim, and a feel for how hard and how straight to strike the ball. Then do backhands. Then alternate.

Third, do the same drill with only one bounce. Try to get more consecutive strikes each time. It's called consistency. Next, try to hit soft overheads into the wall. The ball will bounce right back up into the air, and you can repeat this stoke over and over. This only works if you can control it.

Hit different spins into the wall and watch how they react. Hit the ball different heights and directions. Notice what happens. This teaches you to track and watch the ball better.

Last, you need to know that it's just you and the wall and YOU will never win. There may be a lesson there, too. It is a great workout. It only requires you. It only requires one ball. It is great stress relief. See what creative games you can come up with and enjoy your time alone. Get out there and hit the wall!

Lean In!

originally published July/August 2019

The game of tennis keeps getting faster. Racket and string technologies advance year after year. With each new generation, athletes in general are becoming stronger and faster. Tennis players are no exception, and the size of professional tennis players continues to grow. We average humans have but one defense: Lean in.

You need to realize that the ball is the thing pushing you around the tennis court, and you are bigger than the ball. I've adopted the attitude of "no way that little ball is going to push me back!" You should, too. Leaning in to the ball seems like a simple solution, but so many players have a difficult time doing it. Let's look at some tips to help you lean in.

Start with your attitude. Really get stubborn and realize that getting pushed back is just wrong. It is so hard to hit any kind of shot while moving backward on the court, especially an offensive one. Mentally, think of attacking the ball before it attacks you. Plan to move into the shot rather than just react to it.

Second, make a great split-step, every shot. I make a split-step as my opponent is making contact with the ball. I make my body go forward into the court. This movement enables me to change direction and helps me push forward into the shot. I move diagonally forward so that I can cut off the ball instead of being pushed back by it. The spilt-step sets you up to be offensive when hitting the ball instead of being defensive. It also adds power and depth to your shots.

Third, shorten things up some. Everyone swings too big

sometimes. The technology I spoke about earlier with rackets and strings allows you to shorten your swing and still get great power. A shorter backswing will get you started quicker and allow you to attack even a speeding incoming shot. Then, solid contact is all you need. You've all heard the term, "Use their power against them." Shortening your backswing will help you do just that.

Fourth, follow through. Finishing the shot is more important than starting the shot. That short backswing I want you to take can be very effective if you just finish the shot with authority. A follow-through adds spin and gives the ball speed and direction. Poking at the ball (like I see some of you do) just rebounds the ball wherever. Blocking the ball is too defensive and will get you nowhere. Finish what you start and let your follow-through carry you forward through your shots.

Lastly, use simple commands to get yourself started: "Forward." "Step In." "Attack." "Lean in!"

Which Side Do You Want to Play?

originally published September/October 2019

Tennis is a game of strategy. You all know that, right? Your strategizing should start before you even set foot on the court. I hear people all day asking their partner, "Which side do you want to play?" Usually the answer is, "It doesn't matter to me." I think it matters greatly.

The forehand side and the backhand side as we refer to them are probably named the wrong thing. The deuce side, which most of you call the forehand side, will actually have you hitting more backhands than forehand. Most doubles play occurs up the middle of the court, and since most of you are righties, that means the ball comes to your backhand more when playing on the deuce side. And the ad side, which most of you call the backhand side, is positioned better for you to hit more forehands.

Power is changing the game of tennis, and the big forehand has become a true weapon. On either side you choose to play, you should try to use your speed and good footwork to run around the backhand and hit a more powerful forehand. Set up more to the left before play even starts to open up the forehand side. Stay aggressive when hitting the forehand and keep in mind that it is an extra step or two to get to the ball and then back into position for the next shot. Leave some of the court open and try to tease your opponent into hitting it to your big forehand side.

The real answer to the original question, though, should

always be, "I'll play either side, but I am better on the 'whatever' side." It is true. You play better on one side or the other. I think some people just see the ball better from one side or the other. I absolutely see players that move better on one side versus the other.

Next time you're playing a practice match, try this: Play a set from one side, and the next set, play the other. Pay careful attention to which shots you hit from each side and see which side presents you with more opportunities to hit your favorite shots. Watch your positioning and see which side of the court you cover better. From which side do you step in and move forward better? On which side do you poach more? All are huge factors in choosing which side you "want" to play.

Choose your side wisely!

When Do I Move Forward?

originally published November/December 2019

I am asked daily, "When do I need to move forward?" My answer is, "Almost always!"

In doubles play, it is especially important to control the net. Getting there and staying there are problems for some players. Nearly everyone seems to love to stay back on the baseline and hit ground strokes. Try to recognize when one of your ground strokes pushes your opponent back and notice how much time you have to move forward. Also notice that they often hit a short or weak ball back off your good shot. Most of your problem comes from simply not recognizing when you have pushed an opponent back.

Hopefully you are intentionally trying to get to the net, but also look for weak shots that automatically bring you forward. Examples are a short, slow ball landing inside the service line, a weak floating ball that you could actually take out of the air, or a mishit that needs to be taken advantage of. You can also create opportunity by hitting a wide ball and moving forward. You can hit a lob and use it as an approach shot. You can hit a drop shot and make your opponent hit up on the ball while you are moving forward.

Where do you move to? I think the best net position is one step inside the service line. Closer than that makes you easy to lob over and cuts down your reaction time. Further back than that brings in awkward shots from the infamous "no man's land."

Remember that it may take an extra shot to put the ball away. Don't think you're going to hit a winner every volley.

Control your volley and move your opponents around, making them work and wearing them down. I also like the fact that I can get people frustrated by controlling the net.

Lastly, even though control is a great thing, learn to be aggressive. Put the ball away! That does not always mean hit it harder either. A drop shot is an aggressive shot. A short, sharp angle is an aggressive shot. An overhead is an aggressive shot, even if it is hit slowly to an open area of the court.

Bottom line: Move forward in doubles almost all the time or at least learn to recognize the opportunity. I don't think many of you can win from the baseline in doubles. Singles is a different game altogether, but who plays singles these days?!

What's New in Your Tennis Game

originally published January/February 2020

It's a new year and a new tennis season. I think players get excited about new things. A new forehand. A new backhand. A new racket. New strings. New shoes. New clothing. What's new in your tennis game for 2020?

This upcoming season, try to learn a new shot, whatever you think you are missing in your game. Go see the pros play live. Take a lesson with a teaching professional. Watch a video online. Do whatever you can manage to fit something new into your schedule. Practice your new shot to add a new dimension to your game.

Get a new pair of shoes. You'll be amazed at how comfortable a new pair feels. We tennis players tend to look at wear on the outside of our shoes, but the support on the inside is just as important. Or get a new outfit. My girls said they play better when they're wearing new clothing. The sun is low on the horizon this time of year, so a new hat or visor may be in order.

Get your racket restrung. The rule of thumb is that you restring your racket as many times in a year as you play in a week. Some of you who hit with a lot of spin may need to string more often. Experiment with different strings and tensions. Keep in mind softer strings are better for those who suffer tennis elbow or want to prevent it. I recommend Wilson NXT for the vast majority of my clients.

Get a new outlook. Be more aggressive with your shots. Hit closer to the lines. Hit deeper. Hit it harder. Add spin. These additions are fun and make the game more interesting.

They also make you better at the same time. Changing an attitude can be a major step toward improvement.

I love to teach, but I think players should take lessons from other pros, too. Get new perspectives. Sometimes a pro will say something in a way you haven't heard it before that really clicks.

I do love that pros teach different things and in different ways. Does Roger play the same as Rafa? No way! But I think they teach each other new things all the time, and that is how they've continued to improve.

It's a new season, so get out there and try something new!

Slow Down!

originally published March/April 2020

This is a great tip for everyone arriving to Seaside this spring. It also relates well to your tennis game. Slow down.

My dad had a great saying, "You couldn't wait to miss that, son!" He was right. And you all do it. Tennis shots need to develop, and if you can slow yourself down, it will help you make your shots.

You still need to prepare early. Pick your shot. Commit to it so you can prepare. Get your racket back or in the proper spot for the chosen shot. Then execute, but at the appropriate speed. If you rush, you'll likely miss.

Moving to the ball is obviously crucial. But getting to the ball too early can also be bad. Most of you have the patience of a rabbit, and you also jump around like one. Taking time to step into a shot with balance or step through a volley will aid in your ability to make more shots.

I like my last step into a shot to be aggressive so that I have my body weight behind my shot. I may slow up in the middle on my way to the shot so I can make that last step aggressively. Getting there too early can make you pull off a shot or even change your commitment to a shot. Both are bad things. Slow down.

Finally, finish your shot. Once you choose the shot and execute the shot, make sure you have a full finish. Follow through properly. Return to the ready position. Shuffle back or move to the right spot for the next shot. Slow your mind down to prepare for what's next.

Try some of these tips the next time you're on the court. And for visitors just arriving to Seaside, slow down, you're on vacation.

Watch the Pros Play: How to Improve Your Tennis Game from the Comfort of your Couch

unpublished but was slated for May/June 2020

As I write this issue's article, it is unknown if we'll be back on the courts or staying home and saving lives. Either way, here's a tip on how you can work on your tennis game from your sofa: Watch the pros play. Sports channels are showing classic matches now. Tune in for entertainment and learning.

The television really slows play down. You cannot believe how fast the players are. The court coverage they have is fantastic. You cannot believe how hard they strike they ball. The spin they create is enormous. You cannot believe the work they put forth to win a single point. The angles they hit are unreal. I don't think these things show up on television like they do in person. So, go watch live once the Tour starts back, but for now, what can you learn by watching on TV?

First of all, you get to hear the commentary of the announcers who are former professional players. They'll point out what the players are doing right, what they are doing that's amazing, and what they are getting wrong. But, use your own eyes and watch the match and see what you can figure out for yourself and use in your own game.

Developing the point is done differently by each player. Some are aggressive and try to end the point early. Others are more patient and try to wear down their opponents with consistent play and ball movement. You should know your own strengths and think about how you would apply these strategies into your game.

Positioning is also done differently by each player. Some play near the baseline and catch the ball early, catching the ball on the rise and trying to cut down the reaction time of their opponent. Others play way behind the baseline, trying to take big cuts at the ball and also giving themselves more time to run down balls. You'll need really good speed and conditioning for this style of positioning.

Doubles play is also fun to watch. Notice how teams move together. Take particular notice of starting positions for each point. Watch the movement of the partner not hitting the ball. Doubles is truly a team effort, and even when you are not busy hitting the ball, your movement is important. Movement forward is more important in doubles than in singles. But watch how the forward movement is done in stages instead of an all-out rush to the net. Remember that these athletes move better than we mere mortals.

During your downtime, watch the pros play and find ways to implement their tactics into your game. I can't wait to see you on the courts again! Until then, stay safe and healthy.

Seaside's Tennis Director Commemorates the Program's Best Moments

originally published March 2021

I graduated high school in 1978. Yep, I've been around a while. My high school tennis career was a good one. It was built around wooden rackets and steady ground strokes. Of course, the foot speed I had in those days helped a lot. That too is in the past.

During my college career, tennis was ever-changing. I started and finished my four years with a wooden racket, but the transition to rackets made of aluminum, metal, and other components was rapidly occurring. The change to a serve and volley game was also taking over. With emerging stars like McEnroe, Ashe, and Navratilova having great success with it, my game also changed to this more aggressive style of play.

The great rivalries over the next few decades kept tennis fans immensely entertained: The ground game of Borg versus the net game of McEnroe. Everett's mastery of the baseline versus the athleticism of Navratilova. The return game of Agassi versus the incredible serve of Sampras.

Seaside Tennis itself was started by teaching pros Charlotte and Dave. I arrived in 2000 to take over and put in new programs. Seaside was still an oasis during my first few years. The now surrounding resorts were just getting started, and there truly wasn't a big tennis community at the time. I wondered if I could build this into a program worth staying for.

I remember days when no one would show up for my new morning clinic. Over the years, we built the program to a steady level. Now, you have to sign up in advance to reserve your space. Our Eye-Opener Clinics and Round Robins sell out regularly all year long. I am so happy I endured the lean early years to develop this tennis program. It is successful beyond my wildest dreams.

One of the most exciting events we've held at Seaside Tennis was when Jim Courier did an exhibition with me in 2005. We built a stadium court on the croquet lawn and brought in stands to seat the sold-out crowd. He and I played a round of golf the day before and talked about all the changes tennis had gone through and how it was still changing. He had such incredible insight and shared the changes he thought were coming. I must say, he knew what he was talking about. It was the highlight of my career getting to play with a former world No. 1!

The community of Seaside itself was different then. There were small kiosks in the middle of town center for fun local vendors. The building that houses Great Southern Café now was then called Shades. Bud & Alley's Waterfront Restaurant, my favorite watering hole, was smaller, with J.B. and the Blinders playing music in the upstairs bar most nights. I knew the playlist by heart. It was such a special time in Seaside.

I am so proud of the Seaside Tennis program that I have built. Over my years here, I have met the most amazing people. Most of them come back to see me year after year. Even the ones who aren't currently playing tennis stop by to say hi when they're in town. I have the best clients that any tennis pro ever could ask for.

I'm grateful to be a part of Seaside's history. The Seaside story is ever-changing, and I am happy to be along for the ride.

Seaside Tennis: The Present

originally published June 2021

S easide Tennis presently is in a wonderful place. The last year of Covid-inspired play has been, believe it or not, "good" for tennis. Early in the pandemic, tennis was rated as one of the safest activities you could do. We play outdoors, and it is easy to stay socially distanced on and off the courts. Of course, most of us already knew that, but nothing like a crisis to emphasize how important tennis is to the world.

Currently, Seaside Tennis is busy every day. There is no longer an off season. I really never had much of one anyway since I filled slow times with ladies' groups. Between spring break and summer is a short lull, and we just hosted 25 women from Huntsville, my former stomping ground, for a weekend of tennis drills and round robins. These ladies love their tennis and also enjoy the shops and restaurants in Seaside.

We have added clinics daily to our already robust program. We now have several groups of "tennis friends" that play once or twice or more weekly. I have hired a third pro, and all of us are busy enough to ask for off days. Those are harder to come by than they used to be. And you had better sign up for any Seaside Tennis activities you want in advance from now on or you might not get in.

The past year has taught us many things. We, currently and forevermore, will bring our own towels and water to the courts. There is nothing wrong with a racket "high five" rather than a sweaty handshake at the end of a match. It seems even a little more fun. Why weren't we washing our hands more often? And the pros on Tour have to get their own towels instead of the ball people handling them every time. These seem like good changes to the game of tennis to me. What were we thinking by touching the same water bucket, swapping sweat, and not being as clean as we could?

The present is a good place to be, and the present state of tennis is just fine. Sure, your backhand still needs work, and let's not even mention that service toss. But think of the fun we have on the courts working on these things. I just saw a picture of Lucy, one of my junior tennis players, playing in her first tennis tournament. What a smile she had on her face. That is why I do what I do. My tennis players really enjoy their time on the courts at Seaside. I wouldn't have it any other way.

So, call or come by the shop to book your court, or your clinic, or your round robin, or your lesson. The present holds fun, education, and friendship that we all need to be experiencing right now. Don't dwell on the past or get too far ahead of yourself. Living in the present is a good piece of advice after all. Carpe diem!

A Look into the Future at Seaside Tennis

originally published September 2021

Today is someone's very first day visiting Seaside. I say it all the time. You may have liked it better 21 years ago when I got here or 30 years ago when the town was in its infancy. But the town and entire area is ever evolving and changing. I think it is a great place at *all* these times.

In my last two columns, we talked about tennis at Seaside in the past and today in the present. What about the future? I personally am looking forward to seeing where Seaside goes. I love that I got here in 2000 and am still here today. I love that we have new people coming into the game and I have new players to teach my old tricks to. And I love that I have seen some of my clients, and now friends, almost every year since I began in 2000.

Plans for the future are in play. I hear pickleball courts are coming. I hear a new, improved fitness center is on the horizon. As you have probably already noticed, I now have three young teaching pros working with our guests and residents on their games. Our Ladies Play Day group now has almost 70 players on the list vying to get into that fun morning of match play with lunch (and drinks) afterwards. Our morning clinics are full or almost full every day, and the weekend round robins are even harder to get into.

Although COVID will continue to play a role in our tennis lives, at least in the near future, the future of the game is safe. With so many more people working remotely, tennis will continue to be busy year-round. In the early days of the pandemic, tennis came out as one of the safest activities you could do. That has brought new players into the game. Any newness to any sport always helps it to grow. I brought in new pros for their energy and the different ways they do things. Sports evolve just like towns evolve. I think change is a good thing.

I don't know how many more years I will be here at Seaside. I have had a wonderful time here with you all. I know that the path I have put Seaside Tennis on is a bright one. I know it will always be a fun, happy place. I know that first time visitors to our program will come again and again. And they will tell their friends and family about us. It is growth. I am so proud of it. I will always look forward to the future of Seaside.

Come see me at the courts. Let me introduce you to the new, younger guns I have hired to help Seaside in its future. Let's have more fun moving forward!

CPSIA information can be obtained
at www.ICGtesting.com
Printed in the USA
BVHW091825111121
621363BV00014B/380/J

9 780578 956770